GOOD
INNINGS

GOOD
INNINGS

The Extraordinary, Ordinary Life
of LILY THAROOR

SHOBHA THAROOR SRINIVASAN

PENGUIN
VIKING
An imprint of Penguin Random House

VIKING

USA | Canada | UK | Ireland | Australia
New Zealand | India | South Africa | China

Viking is part of the Penguin Random House group of companies
whose addresses can be found at global.penguinrandomhouse.com

Published by Penguin Random House India Pvt. Ltd
4th Floor, Capital Tower 1, MG Road,
Gurugram 122 002, Haryana, India

Penguin
Random House
India

First published in Viking by Penguin Random House India 2022

Copyright © Shobha Tharoor Srinivasan 2022

All rights reserved

10 9 8 7 6 5 4 3 2

ISBN 9780670096152

Typeset in Adobe Garamond Pro by Manipal Technologies Limited, Manipal
Printed at Replika Press Pvt. Ltd, India

www.penguin.co.in

MIX
Paper from
responsible sources
FSC® C016779

'To describe my mother would be
to write about a hurricane in its perfect power.
Or the climbing, falling colors of a rainbow.'
—Maya Angelou

'My mother was my first country.
The first place
I ever lived.'
—Nayyirah Waheed

For my mother, Lily,
and for women, all of them, always,
who toil, teach, and live each day with fullness.

Contents

Contents

Author's Note

This book is neither a biography nor simply a self-help text with culled dictums for living. I have not approached the writing as a historical account of every year of my mother Lily Tharoor's life. It is, instead, an individual reflection on moments. It is a collection of stories put together from the life of an independent woman who has been a daughter and a wife, and is now still a mother, grandmother and a great-grandmother. It is a recollection formed from personal memories; a narrative of a strong matriarch.

When I was approached by Premanka Goswami of Penguin India to tell my mother's story, I was reluctant to make public the private life of a woman who, as the parent of a national and international figure, would be the subject of scrutiny and ongoing discussion. Premanka persuaded me by saying that the stories and life lessons from someone of my mother's generation are valuable; they are the building blocks and inspiration for the next generation. He is right. These COVID-affected years have been harsh on so many counts. The very fabric of our society and the ways in which we engage with our friends, family and colleagues are continuously challenged. It is in telling our stories, and in hearing stories from others, that we are able to recognize the familiar and feel connected. Sharing memories and moments seem even more vital now, and so I agreed to write this book.

My mother, as she tells us, is a simple woman who was born in a small village in Kerala. She was not 'convent-educated' like her daughters. Her schools were the many places she lived in throughout her life, and her education unfolded through the trials and tribulations of each day. She berates herself for not having invented anything that would be of use to others, and feels her legacy to be lacking. But to us who know her, her distinction is her strong spirit that still endures, her fierce independence that continues in her eighties, sometimes to our frustration, and her constant restless drive to learn and achieve. 'Anything is possible' is her mantra, especially if you have curiosity and a desire to transcend the mundane. And by her independent life she has illustrated that the only ground firm enough to stand on is the one written into existence by her own hand.

My octogenarian mother continues to demand the best and the most out of those she interacts with. She continues to push the next generation to think outside the box. She has now fiercely embraced the Internet and WhatsApp, and she keeps in daily touch with friends and family from multiple continents. Despite her current slow gait, her mind races with a spirit of inquiry; she forwards information and advice daily, and she continues to seek 'the best out of life'. If you ask mummy to sum up her life, she uses a sports metaphor and says, 'I have had good innings'.

In these pages I have used my mother's personal reflections, along with my memories and those of my siblings and her siblings, to build a timeline of an interesting and full life, emphasizing its teachable moments. I start each chapter with aphorisms that inform that section. I hope the narrative will serve as a takeaway for readers who wish to learn or be inspired by the words and stories on the page. I hope that these anecdotes will inspire conversations and action in your own life.

Prologue

Reflections in a Distant Mirror

Shashi Tharoor

This book on my mother, by my sister Shobha, means more to me, as son and brother, than I can put into words.

COVID has transformed our relationship. For the last two years, as I write these words, my mother and I have been living together, as we had not done for any significant period since I went off to college at sixteen. It has been a revelation to me, and I daresay to her as well.

My mother has always relished her independence. Whether it was her insistence, into her eighties, to drive herself on frequent four-hour trips from Kochi, where she lived, to her *tharavad veedu* (ancestral home) in Palakkad district, or in her stubborn refusal to hire full-time domestic help, self-reliance was always my mother's mantra. She doesn't like depending on others' help.

My sisters live abroad. My mother was living alone. For years, I begged and pleaded with her to move in with me, but she always declined. She would come to me for a few weeks at a time and get restless. The reason was simple: she liked being in control, enjoyed her routine, her neighbours. She didn't want to compromise on her autonomy by adjusting herself to someone else's home, someone else's establishment, someone else's environment. So, after a short while with me, almost never longer than a month, she would be off again to resume her own life.

From time to time, my mother would complain to my sisters and me that she felt lonely—but that had always been the case since my father, a larger-than-life dynamo, passed away more than a quarter of a century ago. When COVID struck and began to spread widely in India in mid-March 2020, I refused to let her leave for the airport at the end of a month-long stay in Delhi with me. That temporary change of plan has now become a permanent arrangement. A year after she got 'stranded', as she saw it, in Delhi, she tried to go back to her independent life in Kochi. Within a week, she realized she preferred to be with me. She has been back ever since, and she no longer talks of itching to return to her old life.

Living on her own, Mummy regularly phoned a wide circle of friends and relatives, and met some, preferring them to come to her. She read incessantly and borrowed a wide range of books from a circulating book club. These are things she could, and has, transferred to a new residence, mine, though the books are now from my own eclectic collection. She also used to cook and clean for herself, entertain visitors and manage a household without any full-time help. That she no longer has to do.

My mother's real antidote to boredom is the Internet. She is a tireless emailer and browser of articles, which she forwards widely, and an addict of YouTube videos, which mercifully she has not yet learned to forward. She is active on WhatsApp and is unremitting when it comes to passing on morning greetings, trending videos and, occasionally, 'fake news'. In her time, anything that appeared in print was reliable, and she extends the same credulity to what she reads or hears online. But, offline, her scepticism is her shield.

My mother and I have not always had the easiest of relationships. Which mother and son do? I know my personal and professional journeys have challenged her. And, as I know too well, she is a direct, no-nonsense woman. She can be charming if she wants, but generally doesn't waste time on pleasantries. When others feel the whiplash of her tongue, I shrug apologetically: 'Welcome to the club!'

Growing up, I often felt that nothing I did was good enough for my mother. She had the highest expectations of me, which meant she never allowed me the luxury of self-satisfaction. She rarely congratulated me on any of my prizes or distinctions; they were expected, nothing more.

The result was that she drove me to excellence. She drove me literally, too, to debate and quiz competitions, to All

India Radio to participate in children's programmes, to act in school plays. As the mother of two beautiful daughters, she pressed them to enter the Miss Calcutta contest in 1979. One sister was crowned Miss Calcutta, the other was first runner-up. My mother expected nothing less.

My mother is multitalented but does not stay focused for long. She sings beautifully, but is untrained. A music director who heard her at a party once called her for an audition, but she chose an unwisely high-pitched song and, unused to the studio's sound system, screeched herself out of a playback career. She has tried pottery and ceramics. Every visitor to my home is awestruck by a Ganesh she painted on glass in the Thanjavur style, and yet she has given up painting. I dedicated my 2001 novel, *Riot*, to her: 'tireless seeker who taught me to value her divine discontent'.

Still, she can be determined when she has something to prove. After my father passed away, she single-handedly built a house in the Coimbatore suburbs, overcoming innumerable obstacles, and named it after her childhood home. Her point made—that she could do it—she sold it thereafter.

She disapproved of my entering politics, and prays regularly that I quit and return to what she sees as respectability. But she has queued up to vote for me each time, and when I faced a particularly tough race in 2014, she gamely climbed onto my campaign wagon to show her solidarity and support.

She used to go on vacations with her now mainly octogenarian friends, annually pay tribute to Sathya Sai

Baba's Samadhi at Puttaparthi, and travel widely solo. That's something she is determined to resume when COVID-era restrictions end. She has always embodied the principle that you are only as old as you allow yourself to feel.

As she confidently soldiers on in her mid-eighties, with two titanium knees, both eyes surgically freed of cataracts, but refusing to surrender to age, I feel an admiration welling up for her that I have rarely been able to express before. It has been compounded by a deep-seated revival of love for her that distance and difference had reduced to dormancy. Sharing breakfast, most lunches, and some dinnertimes with her, sitting next to her on the lawn over morning tea and newspapers, sharing sofa space over a drink, jousting over the occasional game of Scrabble or a round of rummy has transformed my own life too.

With my own sons grown up and abroad, as parents of their own children, my mother is now the fulcrum of my existence. Since being widowed eight years ago, I have become accustomed to living alone. Now I never leave home without a farewell kiss to her, never return from an outside engagement without greeting her on arrival. There is a new kind of emotional co-dependence between mother and son that had all but lapsed for nearly five decades.

I grew up thinking of my mother as critical and temperamental. But I failed to see the steel beneath signs of her insecurity, brought on by the ill-health of her husband. Her strength in coping with such an early bereavement, independence of mind and body, faith in herself and determination to face life on her own is an extraordinary lesson. She has earned the right finally to relax, to take love and security for granted and to command the creature comforts she had treated as chores to be fulfilled, not pleasures to be enjoyed. To be the provider of all those for her is a new, and joyous, role for me.

I am lucky to have a mother who sets such an amazing example and who daily gives me the unconditional love only a mother can. This book is the narrative of an 'ordinary life'. But for me there can never be anything ordinary about my mother.

1

Believe in Yourself

'Nothing is impossible. The word itself says I'm possible.'
—Audrey Hepburn

My father was tall and handsome and he was known throughout the village as the person to whose address copies of National Geographic Magazine *and* Reader's Digest *arrived from abroad with regularity. This was not a usual practice in the village where most residents spoke and read only Malayalam. My father was a teacher of History and Geography at Rajah's High School, and he was very well respected in the community. His name was Karat Theyunni Menon, and he was born in 1900, the first year of the new century.*

There were other stories I remember hearing as well—stories of how my father had said that he would only marry after he

1

had his own house. He had grown up in a household of many members, many voices, and many different opinions, and hoped never to bring his own wife back into such a joint family, where she may not have the decision-making opportunities of running a home.

My father's approach to life and living was very modern for the times, and it was expanded by his reading. He was also determined not to start his married life in his wife's tharavad *as was customary in the Nair community with its* 'marumakkathayam'. I remember my mother telling me that the alliance between her and her husband was made carefully. K.T. Menon was selected by Jayashankini's valiyamaman, Ramankutty Menon, who was the eldest male member of the tharavad and thus the Karanavar with important decision-making power. In fact, valiyamaman, was called 'Adhikari Mama' by family members. He was my grandmother's brother and my mother's uncle. K.T. Menon was thought to be a suitable match because of the pedigree of his tharavad, *because he was an educated man and because of his fine features! His economic status and family wealth were not important, as my mother, Mundarath Jayashankini Menon of Elevanchery, was a woman of sufficient means.*

With his schoolteacher's salary, my father bought the house that he wanted in Kollengode. He named it 'Lily Cottage'. In his mid-thirties, he married my much younger mother, the privileged daughter of the well-known Mundarath tharavad, with her long, black, shiny hair and her quick wit and sharp tongue. And, when I was born, first of their nine children, fair like him, and delicate like a flower, he called me 'Lily', even though the official

name on my birth certificate was 'Sulekha'. I was his favourite
child. He was my hero.

Lily was born in the small town of Kollengode in Palakkad
district, Kerala, on 2 December 1935. The British called
the place Kalingudi, or the town of *kollens*. Kollengode was
an unspoiled, beautiful small town and, like many areas in
Kerala, surrounded by fields of rice paddy and dotted with
coconut-laden palm trees. But the town was distinct from
other small towns in the area because of the royal family
who continued to live there, and the folklore that informed
its stories.

Kollengode was known to people all over the Malabar
region of the state because the Kachamkurissi Temple was
located in the vicinity. A visit to the Krishna temple of
Kachamkurissi in Payyallur was thought to be as spiritually
significant to people from Palakkad as a visit to the sacred
Tirupati Temple in Andhra Pradesh. According to legend,
the Kollengode temple site was the place where sage Kashyapa
had seen Lord Vishnu. Thus, Kollengode did indeed have
a sacred reputation. The beautiful Seetharkundu waterfalls
(known to be the waters in which Sita had bathed during
the *vanavasam* with Rama and Lakshmana) was also only a
few kilometres away. Kollengode was a village infused with
beauty and myth.

The Kollengode Kalari Kovilakam that belonged to the
Vengunad chieftains also brought curious and enthralled
visitors from neighbouring areas into the town and gave

the city's residents an immense pride. Despite being a predominantly agricultural area, and located in the grain bowl of the state, there stood a palace in the heart of Kollengode. During the annual Aarattu festival at the Ayyappa Temple, the raja from the Kollengode palace led the procession, carried the main deity and walked through the streets of the town to the water. The procession of men carrying temple *vilakus* was allowed into the palace grounds on that special occasion. In fact, it was said that the Aarattu festival was celebrated well before the Kovilakam had been established in Kollengode and it was, therefore, a duty and privilege of the raja to take on the important role of leading the procession.

Residents of Kollengode looked forward to the pomp and pageantry of a great number of festivals each year. Desavilaku, the annual temple festival of lamps, elephant processions and rituals, was their favourite of these celebrations. There were quite a few temples in Kollengode, and families in the village visited all of them regularly. There were other temples in nearby towns as well, like the Ayyappa Temple in Ootara, and the Shiva temple at Pudugramam. *Archanas* and pujas were performed on special occasions throughout the year and that kept the temples in steady business. Temple visits were, however, as much for socializing as they were to satisfy spiritual callings, and it was the same in Kollengode.

The town centre in Kollengode was a gathering place and gave its denizens an opportunity to meet, socialize and learn about the daily affairs. News of births and deaths, school graduations and new jobs, celebrations and crises spread through the town swiftly, and were shared and discussed, and supported by all. There was a close camaraderie among people in the Nair community. The location was also picturesque: Kollengode was nestled in the foothills of the Annamalai range, and these 'elephant mountains' were visible from all around the city.

In these verdant and spiritual surroundings, Lily's childhood was uncomplicated and comfortable. She was the apple of her father's eye and enjoyed the regard that comes with being the firstborn. While her younger siblings slept on bedding on the floor, Lily had the vaunted position of being the only child to be granted a cot and a mattress (like her parents had) to sleep on.

But she did not grow up spoiled by material comforts. Her mother, Jayashankini, was a progressive woman who had a reformer's outlook of the world. Since she had grown up without want, Jayashankini loaned money liberally and shared food and clothing with those less fortunate. This made her adored by all in the village; but it also meant that, at home, there was less indulgence. Lily grew up seeing her mother save money from household expenses to support the education of the less privileged in the community. That frugality taught her to save as well, and reminded her that it was important to think beyond herself.

Lily also enjoyed the pride and respected status of being her father's daughter. Anyone in Kollengode who required something to be written in English came to her father. He was the resident scribe of the village. People would walk by and see the light of the lantern on his porch still glowing late at night, and they would know that the scholarly man was up late immersed in his reading. Her father's reputation and dignity in the community made Lily feel important.

Lily bloomed in an atmosphere of empowerment and affectionate care. She was deeply pious and prayed to her Guruvayoorappan fervently every day. She believes that he came to her once in the guise of Krishna, with peacock feather and flute, when she was seven. Throughout her life she remained passionate about Lord Krishna. Many years later, when she was living in New Delhi, Lily had the opportunity to visit Mathura, the birthplace of Lord Krishna, and pay her respects to the black-marble idol of Lord Krishna at Dwarkadhish Temple. She felt blessed.

Lily's parents encouraged their children to stand up for their principles and be strong against bullies and firm against injustice. Thus, like her siblings, Lily grew up with confidence. Though she was loving and nurturing in her role as the eldest, Lily was quite capable of standing up to the taunts, tempers and pleas from her siblings even as a child, and so was not easily dominated.

Though she was quiet, Lily had a self-confidence that was unusual for someone her age, especially one brought up in a large family in a small village. As the eldest *chechi*, she had the responsibility of keeping an eye on her younger siblings and she often helped put them to sleep at night. She honed her musical talent by singing soothing lullabies to all of them. Soon everyone noticed that Lily's voice was a gift to the ear, beautiful in sound, and magnificent in range. Though she was never formally trained in music, she remembers that Gopalakrishnan teacher used to come home once a week to give *Ashtapadi* lessons to all the children. These hymns were redolent with meaning and Lily enjoyed them very much.

Lily's voice was soon recognized by all who heard it to be an exceptional one. She was called on to sing at school assemblies and was often asked to lead the choir whenever any dignitaries (such as the renowned poet Vallathol) visited the school for events. She enjoyed this opportunity to perform, and thrived in the attention her singing garnered. She sang without coyness or reserve whenever she was called to represent the school. This enriching experience and the feeling of recognition that comes with visibility built greater self-confidence, and, despite her sheltered upbringing, allowed Lily to enjoy freedom from self-doubt. This was the same confidence that calms the voice within which says 'I can't do it'.

Despite an ordinary childhood, despite the limits of home life, with visits to school and temple as the primary outings, Lily had the conviction and will to break with tradition. Encouraged by her parents, she enrolled for the Kathakali dance group in her school. Kathakali was a classical dance form usually practised by male performers. And it was male dancers who were selected for all the roles, with men donning female attire if the part required it. But Lily was captivated by the movements and mudras of this complex classical dance form and was determined to learn Kathakali. Her inherent confidence spurring her unusual decision, she approached the dance teacher and he allowed her to join the group in school. Soon she was selected to play a part in a Kathakali dance drama in the school's annual cultural show. Lily's powerful performance of Panchali is still remembered by those who had seen her dance that day.

Lily had a driven and restless spirit that dictated that she would not wait for everything to be hundred per cent perfect before she put it out into the world. It was clear that she succeeded because she was willing to move outside her comfort zone and was not afraid to fail.

The most reputable school in Kollengode at the time was Rajah's High School and it enrolled both girls and boys. Lily's parents wanted her to get the best education available and so she was admitted to this co-educational school. The decision says a good deal about her parents' progressive thinking. Soon, with her self-assured spirit and fearless temperament, Lily stood out among her peers. In her tenth standard—the final year before the Secondary School Leaving Certificate exam, she was selected the head girl of Rajah's High School.

Self-confidence is an element linked to almost every aspect of a happy and fulfilling life. Lily's childhood was simple and ordinary, but because she was raised to know that she was valued, that her aspirations were important and that she could study and compete with girls *and* boys, she grew up with a feeling of invincible worth and a 'can do' spirit that she went on to carry with her throughout her life.

2

Childhood Foundations

'Thought creates character.'

—Annie Besant

We didn't have a radio at home when I was a child. Instead, my sisters and I would stand on the porch and watch people come and go on the street. Lily Cottage was on the main road and so we were able to see almost anyone who passed by our house each day.

We were entertained daily by the national news blaring from loudspeakers on bullock carts as they made their way through the town. We would also occasionally hear announcements about the success of the latest films that were playing in the makeshift 'cinema talkies'—drummers on the street would announce the highlights of the blockbuster that was still 'houseful' even in its third week at the local cinema! We also looked forward to the chorus of calls during Karkada Sankranti. *'Chetta po, shivodi va.' This was the time of year when everyone cleaned out their homes and discarded all the broken pots and pans and other rubbish that had accumulated. Domestic staff would gather these items in palm leaf baskets and walk far away to discard the contents. This 'spring cleaning' was performed the day before the first day of the Malayalam month of Karkada when the goddess Bhagvati was invited to homes in Kerala. In the days that followed (and sometimes for the entire month) the Ramayana is read aloud at home. One Karkada Sankranti my mother bought me an idol of Lord Krishna for my puja corner. I had been pleading for a Krishna idol for a very long time.*

Another memory I have from my childhood was watching my father count his earnings from a paddy sale after the harvest. My father had become a teacher's trainer by then and he did not have the time to supervise all the paddy fields that belonged to my mother. But, as the man of the house, he was expected to help manage my mother's krishi, *despite his other responsibilities at school.*

At that time, the family owned most of the rice paddies that surrounded the tharavad. *Mundarath tharavad was the most important and prominent household in Elevanchery. It was occupied by Jayashankini's valiyamaman and his family even though the home belonged to Jayashankini. Stored in the attic were 11th-century copperplate inscriptions, granting the ownership of vast lands around Elavanchery to the Mundarath family. The house was by far the grandest in the area. It was unusually built in English style, with a closed roof, instead of the familiar interior courtyards seen in the* naalukettu *or* ettukettu *of traditional Kerala houses. Although the earnings from my mother's inheritance was more than enough for the family's upkeep, my father was too proud to use his wife's wealth for his personal needs. When he had to examine the paddy fields or supervise the* karyastan, *he walked all the way from Kollengode to Elevanchery, a 7-kilometre distance, just to save the few annas it would have cost him to ride the bus. I suppose some of my thrift and reluctance to spend money on my own needs comes from these early observations of my father's behaviour.*

We passed our days in simple ways. I was very tall and some tears were shed, until I was older and realized the value of a good height. I used to come home from school and cry for having to stand at the back during assembly because I was too tall to be in the front row. But there were happy moments as well. We enjoyed the simple activities around us. My sisters—Bhanu, Renu—and I used to while our spare time watching large groups of goats being led by the goatherd for transfer or sale, or we stared for hours at cows on their way to the pozha *(lake) for a bath. This was actually very entertaining! The goats especially had a restless personality and required many clever manoeuvres from the goatherd to coax the group to stay together. Their playful nature was fun to watch.*

Another exciting detail I remember from those days were the many convoys of foreign soldiers who passed by on their way to some other place. This was during the war and I suppose that they may have been British Army soldiers. The soldiers would throw biscuits and wrapped bread from their tall trucks and we would all jump to catch the treats if they'd fall close enough to where we were standing.

I was called Nani kutty often at home. It was my father's mother's name and my muthashi was always fond of me. I believe that name was given to me on my chorunnu, *while putting the first ball of rice into my mouth. It was only in school that I was called Sulekha. So, I had multiple names like many children today. And it is such a coincidence that my American great-granddaughter, Mrinalini, is also called Nani by many people.*

I did not have a lot of friends but that was common back in those days. Coming from large families, we would mostly play with our brothers and sisters, and chat with the neighbourhood children when we were all assembled around the same time in our porches and front muttams. Among all my cousins, I was close to my paternal cousin, Mani, as we studied in the same school and her house was not far from ours. At home, my sister, Renuka, and much younger brother, Gopanunni, were my favourite siblings. They were sweet in temperament and very attached to me so I spent more time with them during the day. I recall making up stories and relating them to Renuka. The stories were imagined- about train journeys and travel. But I did not write them down into a notebook because my script on the page was so illegible. Isn't it funny that I was named Sulekha but my handwriting is not at all beautiful? I also used to sing to my siblings regularly, and many of them became wonderful singers as well.

Lily's childhood was pleasant. She was the first granddaughter her paternal grandparents were gifted with and she was made to feel that she was her Muthashi's favourite. Her father's mother treated her as a special grandchild and asked her to visit often. When she was older and in high school, Lily would be allowed to make the monthly excursions by bus to her paternal home to watch visiting troupes perform Kathakali. Sometimes she would drop in just for a quick visit. She often went with Bhanu, the sister closest to her in age. Since Lily's mother had lost her own mother soon after her birth, the indulgences of a maternal grandmother were unknown to Lily and her siblings. However, their regular visits to their father's tharavad made up for it and was something they would look forward to.

By the time Lily was twelve or thirteen, her father was promoted with a higher pay for training other teachers at school. Lily recalls her experience of enjoying one of its perks—going to the Perungottakavu Temple in Nemmara in a taxi! In fact, there would be occasional taxi rides to the cinema theatre to watch a movie as well.

Lily was not an academic star and her performance was more 'satisfactory' than 'exceptional'. It was her creativity and cleverness that made her stand apart, in addition to her loving and patient demeanour with the very young siblings. Lily was in awe of the importance her father held as Kollengode's scribe and thought of the art of writing as a special talent. Lily's voice was exceptional as well, which she further strengthened while singing for her little brother

Aniyan every night. Aniyan remembers that he often cried for his chechi if she was not there at bedtime. As the eldest, Lily also helped her mother by keeping an eye on her brother, Mohanan, who was severely disabled and immobile, and was unable to communicate or do much on his own. Sadly, he did not live long and died when he was only nine. Lily remembers Mohanan as a beautiful boy who used to make a grunting sound when he was happy. His lively eyes would follow his mother's movements with a wide smile. Lily spent most of her childhood years with her siblings, helping her mother at home, or attending school. As Rajah's High School was becoming a well-known institution, formidable personalities like the great poet P. Kunhiraman Nair came to teach at the school. Lily's brother, Gopanunni, was, in fact, taught by the poet in school. P. Kunhiraman Nair lived in a rental house opposite the Kollengode Railway Station and his creative prowess was soon noticed by the people of the town. Several years later, the same Kunhiraman Nair, now the great Mahakavi P, recipient of the prestigious Sahitya Akademi Award, would happen to visit Lily and her family in Calcutta and appreciate her son Shashi's literary talents.

There was something Lily enjoyed the most—praying. The time she spent in prayer was important to her as it kept her focused, grounded her, and nurtured her spiritual well-being. She felt that the more connected she was to Guruvayoorappan, the better prepared for life she would be. She believed that her devotion would allow her to make the correct decisions and qualify her to explain the mysteries of life that confused most people. Prayer to her was a form of service, a discipline and commitment that she practised through her regular hours of worship and visits to the temple wherever she lived. She drew her strength from her faith in God.

3

Spread Your Wings

'You can't cross the sea merely by standing and staring at the water.'

—Rabindranath Tagore

I was allowed to walk to school without a chaperone by the time I was in high school. I usually walked with the other girls my age who also attended my school. My mother bought me a pair of slippers as she thought that I was finally old enough to own one. I wore them excitedly whenever I had the occasion to walk anywhere. We were a colourful group of girls—in our bright pavada davinis *with identical long plaits tied in red ribbons that swung on our backs as we walked with our books in hand. Back in those days, I was fond of wearing a bright red* pottu *on my forehead. My mother, however, accused me of 'dressing up too much' for school and courting attention. So, I ended up wearing only a small black dot on my forehead as a pottu.*

Sometimes there were boys in step behind us; they'd join only as we'd turn the corner of the road, out of the view of our watchful mothers. Those times were different. We did not really have a chance to speak to boys other than in the classroom (which had strict rules of silence), so interactions with boys were usually limited within family members and relatives. I was raised strictly and, as I look back, it is funny how I used to think that the act of holding hands with a man and sharing a kiss was how babies were conceived! What we had in our times was an innocent friendship and we broke no rules and there was no 'fooling around'.

Despite my modesty and proper behavior throughout, it was in my youth that I was unfortunately subjected to a scandal. I was in the tenth standard when the local paper, Thaniniram, *headlined that K.T. Menon and Jaishankini Amma's daughter, Sulekha, was 'turning boys' heads and leading them astray with her beauty and her tantalizing ways'. My respectable parents were shocked and upset. It was discovered much later that a humiliated fellow, who had asked my father for a loan but had been turned down, had decided to cause trouble and teach my father a lesson. The fellow had paid someone to write a mean story in the paper to embarrass my parents. But before the truth was known by my parents, my mother had already decided that, to protect the family name from further discredit, she would find me a groom as soon as I completed the SSLC examination. The end of my schooling had been determined. I was to be married at the earliest!*

Lily's paternal uncle was married to Yeshoda, a schoolteacher from the Tharoor tharavad in the neighbouring village of Chittlamchery. Besides knowing the Tharoor family as a respectable local Nair tharavad, Lily's parents were also related to them by the marriage of her uncle. Sadly, the Tharoor family had had the misfortune of losing their primary bread winner. So, when Karthiayanee Amma's husband, Kandar Nair, passed away at a young age, leaving her with eight children to raise on her own, the eldest son, Parameshwar, who was Yeshoda's older brother, took on the role of family provider. Parameshwar first travelled to Bombay as a stenographer, and then, because of his hard work and sheer dint of ability, became an executive in several British establishments. One British company had sent him to London to earn a living that would make it easier to support his entire family. In a few years, Tharoor Parameshwar had made a little money and had created the right opportunities to take his three younger brothers, Chandran, Bhaskaran and Krishnan, back with him to the UK. He wanted to make sure that they too could make their way in the world and support the family. In 1952, Param, as he was affectionately called, now over thirty and in his prime, came back home to get married. The news of a local wedding was the talk of the village. The most exciting detail was that the bride was from Kollengode; and, coincidentally, she was also named Lily! Plans were made for Param and Lily to get married in Kerala and then move to Calcutta to start married life together.

This story is important because it sets the stage for *our* Lily's marriage. Lily remembers Parameshwar visiting her parents when he came to Kollengode before his wedding to seek their blessings. He was greeted and served with tea in the guest house that her father had built on the grounds of Lily Cottage. By then they had outgrown the original dwelling and had to expand the house to accommodate the growing family.

At Parameshwar's wedding, the Chittlamchery family noticed that K.T. Menon's eldest daughter had grown up to be a young woman who was beautiful and tall, an inch taller than Param's younger brother Chandran, for whom they were looking for a bride. The next family wedding was already in their minds. In 1955, the young and dashing twenty-five-year-old Chandran was sent a studio portrait of our Lily to London, and Lily was probably shown a photograph of Chandran. It didn't take time for the couple to agree to their parents' wishes. That was how marriages were fixed in those days!

In the January of 1955, Chandran Tharoor wrapped up his seven years in London and returned to India to settle down.

Chandran's first excursion after arriving in Kerala was to go to Kollengode to meet Lily. As he had expected, he was charmed by her instantly. She was a beautiful girl with large expressive eyes and a confident smile. Her integrity was apparent despite her silence. Lily was impressed as well with Chandran's friendliness, twinkling eyes, warm smile and easy conversational style. Dressed smartly, he was quite different from anyone she had seen or met before. Her meeting with

Chandran excited Lily and the idea of an early marriage no longer seemed like the punishment which she had expected it to be. In fact, it was more like a reward. Marriage would give her an opportunity to leave the confines of the small town and explore a new place. It would allow her to spread her wings and be independent and free of house rules and protocols. Marriage was becoming an easy concept to embrace. The families confirmed the marriage and fixed the date. Chandran was now officially allowed to pay a visit to see his bride-to-be whenever he wanted. He would stop by for an hour on each visit and the young couple began to get to know each other.

On 2 February 1955, Lily and Chandran were married on the *muttam* of Lily Cottage in the presence of their family and a few friends. It was a small, intimate wedding. Lily recalls sadly that nobody took any photographs that day. Once she was married that changed; the formal family picture taken at a professional studio, marking the growing years of the children, would become an annual family tradition that Chandran and Lily followed in whichever city they lived. The framed portraits of the children—until they dispersed to college—still decorate the walls of Mundarath House today.

Lily would soon leave her parents' home for her new life. Plans had been made to travel to Calcutta where Chandran was joining the *Amrita Bazaar Patrika* as an Advertising Executive. They were to stay at Lily and Param's house while looking for a rental home for themselves. Armed with suitcases and accompanied by a Malayalee housemaid hired in Elevanchery, they arrived in the bustling capital of West Bengal. But something else awaited them when they arrived—an offer from London in the form of an appointment letter. This was unexpected and life was about to change in a big way.

'You can adapt to anything' was Lily's mantra. It's a lot easier said than done for many; but knowing, subconsciously perhaps, that things can always get better kept her mind open for new opportunities. Lily had an adventurous spirit, a curious mind, and a quest for new experiences. She was not afraid to challenge conventions or adapt to changes if things were not convenient. With a like-minded partner in Chandran, she was ready for a new life and all that it had to offer!

4

Embrace the Unexpected

'You have to take risks. We will only understand the miracle
of life fully when we allow the unexpected to happen.'
—Paulo Coelho

I left the sheltered life of a small town in Kerala for the big city of
Calcutta soon after my wedding. It was a time of anticipation—
the newness of a man and a marriage, and the excitement of not
knowing what would happen in the days ahead. But, within
a week of my arrival in the city, my husband announced that
his former boss had written him a letter, offering him a better
position in London. What a surprising twist of fate! Chandran
was excited but I, at first, was confused. The maidservant would
have to be sent back to Kerala and we had to apply for a passport
for me since I had never had one. But Chandran reassured me.

He was always one for positive thinking. He converted the first-class plane ticket sent to him by his employer into two economy tickets for a flight to London. We used the extra money for winter clothes that we knew we would soon need. I feel that this surprising and sudden turn of events marked the beginning of the unusual life that I would continue to live for the coming years.

London and my new life had its ups and downs. Despite the excitement of being in a foreign land, I was lonely and missed India. My English was not good. But my husband was kind and loving. He would cook all the meals in the early days since I had never cooked before. Even when I tried to cook, my initial attempts in England were not very successful. He would also wash our clothes by hand and take care of most of the domestic duties before taking the bus to work. He was gentle and patient and spoiled me a lot. The only time he would tease me was when he commented on how long it took me to eat my meal. He would cook me breakfast, take the bus to work, telephone from the office after his early appointments, and I would still be toying with my breakfast at the time. Even today, I take longer than most people to eat my meals!

But, despite all my husband's help, my lack of conversational skills was a problem and I knew that I would need to learn English if I wanted to feel independent or wished to exit the flat for anything. Those days, there were few Indians in London to take me under their wing. But we had a radio at home, so I decided that I would listen to radio programmes and mimic the conversations that I heard. In fact, much of the English that I learned to speak in London was by imitating the sound and the words of the host, Roy Plumley, on Desert Island Discs. He interviewed movie stars and celebrities about 'the soundtracks of their life'. My children tell me that, even after all these years, the show remains popular and still continues to air with other hosts.

I also learned the bus routes so that I could visit my husband if I needed to, run errands, and later take my son for doctor visits when my husband was away at work. I knew how important it was to learn the routes so that I was not too dependent.

Chandran returned to London with Lily to work for the *Amrita Bazaar Patrika* newspaper. There were only three Indians—all Bengalis—who also worked with him. Everyone else was British. The office was on Fleet Street where most of the British national newspapers were housed. Fleet Street was

the centre of the printing and publishing world in London, and a thrilling place to be for Chandran. He was happy to be back in London and was looking forward to introducing the city and all of its charms to his new wife.

Life in London was fun at first. Lily enjoyed being married, being doted on, being the 'queen of her castle' and she had fun checking out the new

Chandran Tharoor,
Newspaper Executive

fashions that were so different from what she had had in Kollengode. She cut off her long hair and got it 'permed'; she wore skirts and trousers; she discovered bus routes and learned to travel short distances on her own. She was often asked by strangers on the bus if she was an 'Italian'. She was pleased to hear such comments as they validated her success in adapting to western ways smoothly.

Chandran was an attentive husband, and a supportive, affectionate and understanding man. As a newspaper employee he had invitations to important events. Lily remembers that she attended a tea for journalists and their wives soon after she arrived in London. She was seated at the same table as Lord Mountbatten. She wrote about it with much excitement to her parents.

On the weekends, they made time for short outings. They often took the bus to Trafalgar Square and stood below Nelson's statue where Lily would delight in the hundreds of pigeons that fearlessly swooped down for crumbs. When the weather was warm, they went for walks and ate fish and chips. The fish was greasy and wrapped in newspaper which, she noticed, would be well soaked up in oil before they finished eating. Sometimes, when they had saved enough, they went to the cinema. She enjoyed her new life as long as it wasn't so bitterly cold and damp.

But Lily's mind sought a purpose and she felt restless. Coincidentally, change was around the corner once again. It had only been a few months since their marriage when she learned that she was pregnant. Chandran was thrilled. They would soon become parents. Despite the homesickness, Lily looked forward to the new baby and all the joy that parenthood could bring. She would also have more to do with her time, she thought.

Meanwhile, in the new office building, Chandran had become close friends with Mr Andrae, an older gentleman who represented six media outlets. Mr Andrae became a considerate friend to Lily as well. Lily remembers taking the number 19 bus from Fulham, where they lived when she was expecting Shashi, to Fleet Street, where the office was located. She would take the bus often during her pregnancy and visit Chandran and have lunch with him and Mr Andrae. She remembers that Mr Andrae was very kind and would insist that she eat the grapes that he had bought 'for nourishment in her delicate condition' and would make sure that she rested in his office with her feet up before returning home on the bus.

On 9 March 1956, Shashi was born at the Royal Free Hospital in Islington. He was born on Mahashivratri night, and the name Shashi was decided as a reference to the crescent moon on Lord Shiva's forehead. So was it with the name Chandrasekhar—Chandran's full name. Lily insisted on adding 'Krishna' as a middle name, along with 'Theyunni' after her father. So, Lily and Chandran's son's full name on the birth certificate was Shashi Krishna Theyunni Tharoor. He was fair and light-eyed, and the nurses exclaimed that he 'looked like an English baby'. Lily and Chandran were over the moon with their son's birth. Shashi was adored by his young parents.

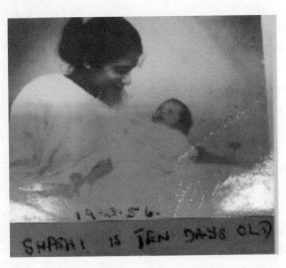

When Shashi was two months old, *The Statesman* got in touch, and Chandran was offered a new job and a better opportunity. This was quite impressive for a still young journalist as *The Statesman* was managed by a British corporate group in those days. Ownership of *The Statesman* was only transferred to corporate groups in India in the mid-1960s, when Nani Palkhivala became the first Indian chairman.

The Statesman's office was small: two employees, with one London correspondent, James Cowley, and Chandran Tharoor in charge of all the advertising and administrative duties. The position, therefore, had more responsibility and more autonomy, and was definitely an opportunity for career growth for Chandran. There was a new baby in the house, and the additional salary that came with the better job was also useful. Lily felt that her son had brought them luck. It had only been a year and three months since their marriage, and Chandran had been offered this far better position.

But their life in London was not easy. Not only did Chandran and Lily not have family or help, but they also didn't have access to a washing machine and there was no central heating at home. These were difficult post-war days and Chandran worked around the clock to make it easier for Lily. He washed the baby's cloth diapers by hand, and did much of the cooking before he left home in the morning for work. Yet, it seemed like their days were full of undone chores. In addition to their own housework, Chandran's warm-heartedness and generosity meant that all his bachelor friends from India, who had recently moved to England (and were still settling in), took their refuge in Chandran and Lily's home. Though the company of friends was enjoyable, there was much more work to do with the additional guests at home. Shashi was a toddler, susceptible to colds in the damp English weather, and he required a lot of attention. To make matters worse, the landlady expected tenants to have spotless windows every week when she came to inspect the flat and complained about Shashi's cries and suggested that crying babies were a disturbance to other tenants!

The excitement of living in the big city of London eventually wore off as the weather turned colder, and Lily's desire to return to India deepened. More than her homesickness was the feeling that life would be so much easier back in India. So, when Chandran heard of an amazing opportunity to move to Bombay as the Bombay Manager of *The Statesman* newspaper, he did not hesitate to submit his application. Fortunately, his application was successful. Chandran Tharoor was soon to be the man in charge in

Bombay. They booked their way back to India on the passenger ship, *Circassia,* and left London two and a half years after Lily had first arrived on England's shores. Shashi was only twenty-one months old at that time.

We know that we need to learn to adapt in order to 'grow' and move forward in life. Many of us resist change because we fear we will not be able to adapt to the new ways. We sometimes believe we will lose something of value if we make a change. Change, after all, affects our daily routines, and it is that routine and the comfort of a familiar structure that makes most of us feel secure.

Despite her childhood in the small town of Kollengode, her lack of fluency with the English language, or the unfamiliarity with western etiquette or rules, Lily made the changes demanded of her to the best of her abilities. She learned this new language by her creative persistence with the radio programming. English was, in fact, only the first of many languages that she would teach herself. Furthermore, she had even adjusted her palate to different cuisines. The weather and domestic work were not easy to embrace, but the experience helped grow and reshape her thinking.

Lily had a spirit of adventure embedded in her nature. She was driven by hope and excitement rather than by anxiety or anger. She was also practical and sensible and had strong instincts about opportunity. And, though this sojourn abroad was a short one, and though it seemed like she was more dependent than self-sufficient, she had lived differently and it had changed her in many ways. Her years in London and her exposure to the western way of living built the foundation for the self-reliance she would count on later in life.

5

Moving Back. Moving Forward

'The future depends entirely on what each of us does every day; a movement is only people moving.'

—Gloria Steinem

We returned to India on the passenger ship Circassia *in December 1957. It took us about three weeks to reach the port. The Statesman had sent us back in style, and I remember the journey as a wonderful experience. We played 'Housie-Housie' (Bingo) on the ship. Once when Chandran and I were playing for a large cash prize, I only had one number to win the full house. Just as another number was about to be called out, a ship steward came and insisted that I must attend to my crying baby in the cabin. I got up and rushed off to attend to my son. When I returned after settling him back to sleep, I discovered that they had already called my number and I had won the full house a long time ago. Unfortunately, the prize had gone to a later claimant. This reinforced my belief that things that needed to be done had to be done in a timely way. Opportunities should not be squandered.*

We had to dress up in fancy clothes for mealtimes. The dining rooms on the ship were grand and stylish, and formal place settings were used for the guests when they came to dinner. I was quite impressed when uniformed waiters presented us engraved menu cards from which we had to select our meals. My husband and I walked on the deck and mingled with others in a grand ballroom where dancers in white tuxedos and long dresses twirled around. I wore my saris and people turned to look at me. Even though I'm a bit of a clumsy sari-wearer, everyone looks beautiful in a sari.

I remember there was a passenger who was an Indian Navy Captain returning from an assignment in London. His name was Sourendra Nath Kohli and he soon became our friend. Kohli would spend time with us every day, and play with Shashi often. Once when he was carrying Shashi, our son accidentally soiled Kohli's spotless uniform. Years later, Chandran and I would share this story with our children at home. Sixteen years later, when Shashi was getting the University award on St Stephen's College Founder's Day, S.N. Kohli, who had been an alumnus of the college himself, was invited as the chief guest to distribute the awards. When Shashi went up on to the stage for his award, he recalled this incident from his childhood. Admiral Kohli laughed as he shook Shashi's hand. What a wonderful coincidence it was for my husband and I to meet our old friend after all these years!

As soon as we arrived in India, and before my husband took charge of the Bombay office, we went to Kerala so that we could introduce Shashi to my parents, in-laws and to the rest of the family. Everyone was excited to meet the 'foreign-returned' members of the family. As Shashi was a picky eater, I wanted to make sure that he was not without the food he was used to eating in London. So, we had travelled back to India with many bottles of Marmite and Bovril in our suitcase. My sisters and brothers still tease me that I spoilt my son by ordering food shipments from England even after we had settled into the rhythm of life in Bombay. When I think of it now, the purchase does not only seem like an extravagant mother spoiling her son, but also silly, because the main ingredients in Bovril were beef stock and bone broth. Shashi has been a strict vegetarian ever since he was old enough to know what he was eating!

In the three years that I was away, my parents had moved from Kollengode to my mother's tharavad 'Mundarath' in Elevanchery. The decision was a practical one as my valiyamaman (great uncle) had passed away and the house that belonged to my mother required upkeep that she could now offer. All my brothers and sisters were born by then and the increase in family members meant that Lily Cottage was not big enough for them. My father had also retired from his job. My parents rented the home in Kollengode to a schoolteacher, and moved to the tharavad with my younger siblings.

I was disappointed to return to Elevanchery and not Kollengode which had been my childhood home. Kollengode is still my cherished place in Kerala. I have so many fond memories of growing up there. But Mundarath House was a huge, beautiful and comfortable property. It was also a pleasant change to have so much space to live in after our life in a small flat in London. Unlike most of the tharavads in Kerala, Mundarath was built like a large mansion with a European design. The rooms were larger and more spacious than in a nalukettu. We had a dining room and a wrap-around porch where we could sit and enjoy the morning and evening breeze.

Shashi and Lily stayed in Mundarath for about four months as Chandran set up the office in Bombay and organized their living arrangements. Mr Pluck, who had been *The Statesman's* manager for many years, took a very long time to vacate the flat and pack up his belongings. Finally, after what seemed like an eternity, Chandran was able to say that the flat was ready and his wife and son could join him in Bombay. Chandran had been staying with his brother and his *edathiamma* and their two sons in a flat in Worli while the flat was being readied. He too was eager to start his own life with Lily and Shashi.

Lily arrived in Bombay to discover that their new home was also her husband's new office! This was a potentially useful change in lifestyle. Chandran had taken over the fourth floor of Kasturi Building and created an interesting set-up: the place used to be a huge five-bedroom flat of which two bedrooms were converted to an office for the manager, with a reception area and a cubicle for the Bombay correspondent. The remaining three bedrooms and kitchen would serve as the residence. The home and the office were separated by an iron gate that usually kept the two establishments distinct and apart.

Chandran's new job came with a company car allocation as well: a Landmaster car made by Hindustan Motors. It was the precursor to the famous Indian car—the Ambassador. They were both thrilled to have a vehicle for their personal use. It was the first time that Lily would have a car of her own! She was proud of her husband. He was only twenty-eight and was the first Indian manager of *The Statesman* in Bombay.

Kasturi Building was the Bombay branch-office building of *The Hindu* newspaper and was a well-known landmark. Located near Churchgate Station, it was at the heart of the city. The city beacon—LIC building—was opposite, and Bank House, where author and poet Kamala Das lived, was only a short walk away. Lily and Chandran were surrounded by interesting and kind neighbours who were

warm and welcoming. They had company when they wanted to socialize, and the support and friendship of people in a new city was a blessing. Chandran loved the vibrant energy of Bombay and thrived in his new position.

Lily took to Bombay like she took to every new experience. As the wife of a 'media man', she needed to learn to 'throw parties' and entertain guests regularly at home. She enjoyed social gatherings and the thrill of new experiences so she embraced entertaining easily. The company allotments for the home were opulent. She remembers having winter curtains which were made of a heavier fabric than the summer sheers. The curtains had to be changed when the weather changed. The practice of changing drapery was really just a 'show' as it was only a few degrees cooler in winter in Bombay, but such was the British style! They also now had fancy cutlery that she had to learn to use correctly, including forks with serrated tines for grapefruit and an assortment of liqueur and sherry glasses that Chandran washed and dried meticulously on his own and stored away after every party.

All these customs and ceremonies were new to Lily and quite different from the life she had been accustomed to until then. With his own initiative, Chandran applied and secured a membership at the Bombay Gymkhana Club, which was a prestigious leisure club once exclusively for British citizens. Lily and Chandran felt like they were a part of a dynamic and progressive new world.

Lily enjoyed dressing up, adopting new fashions and trying new hairstyles. She remembers that she wore a sleeveless sari blouse with trousers on one occasion and turned heads at the club. Someone asked her sarcastically if she was starting a new fashion. She may have protested at the question when it was asked, but, soon, she noticed other women adopting the sartorial style. Lily was a trendsetter! She had an inner confidence that told her she was quite special and exceptional.

Chandran was very interested in politics and was committed to being informed daily of the current events and news. He often spoke about the state of the country and had opinions about public policy and its implementation. He subscribed to three daily newspapers in English and an additional Malayalam paper, *Mathrubhumi*, for Lily to read. Lily was not all that interested in political analysis in the English dailies, but the *Date Book* that announced the weekly city engagements, the interesting stories in the *Middle*, the spiritual reflections in *Speaking Tree* and the sections in the paper about achievements and trends—all of these interested and impressed her the most.

One day, when she was skimming through the *Times of India,* she read an article that mentioned a Films Division Corporation of India (FDCI) office on Peddar Road. She knew that Peddar Road was in South Bombay and not too far from where they lived, so when she found out that they were in the business of voice-over work, Lily took herself to the Films Division Office and announced that she was interested and available for voice-overs in Malayalam. Whether it was her chutzpah or being in the right place at the right time that got Lily what she wanted one will never know, but she was soon dubbing in Malayalam for Films Division.

The work that she did and the contacts she made through Films Division Corporation led her to All India Radio where she was immediately brought on to do Malayalam interviews with dignitaries from Kerala who visited Bombay. In a few months, Lily Tharoor had made a mark with her confident questions and voice, and it was only a short time before Mr Vaanamali, Bombay talent scout, 'discovered' her.

Lily recalled that whenever clients had a job in Malayalam, Mr Vaanamali got in touch and soon the voice-over for the project was assigned to her. She recorded many advertisements, but it was the lilt and charm of her compelling 'koodi koodi varuntha lavanyam' commercial that the children still recollect in their family stories. This ad in Lily's voice invited the user to lather up with a particular soap that guaranteed lustre and loveliness in its user.

Lily's voice-overs, dubbing work for films, and interviews for All India Radio kept her busy and content. In her own words, she 'had a full life'. As there was a maidservant from Kerala to help in the house, Shashi and the home had the attention that they required to thrive as well.

Success has its own reward and encourages the successful person to continue to achieve. Lily's inner mantra was 'time was not to be squandered; every minute in the day had to count for something'. She also believed that it was every person's duty to make the most of themselves. Successful people have a purpose. Lily had a purpose. As a result, she was excited, passionate and fearless. And successful people usually love to show their passions to others. As Lily would say to her husband, and later to her children, 'have a focus in life'. If you've found something that inspires you, and makes you excited to get up, get out, and achieve, then you're successful, regardless of what other people think.

Lily lived life *her* way—and that to her was the best sign of success there is. Perhaps it was also because she had a restless soul or, as she herself says, 'I am too ambitious'. But these very qualities made her reach out beyond prescribed roles and tasks.

6

Learning from City Life

'I have not ceased being fearful, but I have ceased to let fear control me.'

—Erica Jong

I enjoyed living in Bombay and was very happy to have Chandran close by in his office across the hall. The staff, the car and the annual holiday allowances to travel to see my parents made us extremely happy. By the time our third child was born, our yearly travel perks included an allowance for airplane travel for the entire family. My husband's career growth improved our lives as well.

The city was an exciting place. I enjoyed the vitality of Crawford Market where everything, from vegetables to clothes, could be bought easily, and I could bargain with the salesmen for a reasonable price. There were hardly any things that were not available in this wholesale market. And, anything that could not be bought in Crawford Market could be bought at the Sahakari Bhandar near Regal Cinema. This co-operative shop offered convenience, good quality and a regular availability of products that I had soon become familiar with. The shop would do home deliveries as well. City life had so many conveniences!

I was excited when I learned that I was expecting for the second time. We had always wanted more children and I really wanted a daughter. We had waited to have another child until we were settled in Bombay, but now we were ready. And then Shobha was born! She was such an easy baby that even her delivery only took a few minutes. My mother came to Bombay to help us for a few months. Shobha was a quiet infant who, instead of crying, soothed herself by sucking her two fingers. Friends in the building called her 'little Cleopatra' because of her large, light-brown eyes and thick, dark hair. She didn't crawl at six months like other children but pushed herself on her bottom all over the house. My brother, Unni, was living with us and doing his MA those days, and Shobha would scoot to him in this strange sliding manner and expect to be picked up. He was very fond of her.

When Shobha was still an infant, I discovered that I was expecting again. What a surprise! This was a difficult delivery because the baby was much bigger; but soon we had another lovely baby girl in the house. We named her Smita—the 'ever smiling' one—to match the other names starting with 'S'. Smita had a very distinct personality. She was friendly and talkative and not shy like Shobha and she provided a lot of entertainment to family and friends. My days and heart were full.

A fun memory from those years is our Amul Story. Early in 1961, Amul's advertising agency, ASP (Advertising & Sales Promotion Ltd) was looking for a face to launch their baby milk powder. It was a first-of-its-kind ad campaign and the creative team had travelled all over the country searching for the baby face that they wanted to represent their new product. The cameraman for this campaign was Shyam Benegal. Shyam was a young man and wasn't yet the big name he is today. He had taken many photos but the team hadn't found the face they wanted. Then, one day, ASP's creative head, Sylvester da Cunha, asked my husband (they were friends and had co-founded the Advertising Club in Bombay), 'You also have a baby, don't you?' My husband showed him the picture of our ten-month-old Shobha; photos were taken, and the rest, as they say, is history! Shobha became the first ever Amul baby. The campaign was in black and white and ASP recorded Shobha's selection in an ad in the trade press that announced '712 shots before this one!'

Shobha

A year later, when ASP was looking for a face for the

43

ad-campaign with colour pictures, they picked our younger daughter, Smita. Smita's smiling round face and chubby cheeks were perfect for the campaign. Her adorable portrait was on the walls of so many chemists all over the city. We even saw the photo hanging on the walls of a chemist in Calcutta many years later.

Smita

Life was busy with three children at home. My husband, whose early years had been spent in London, thought that it was important for his son to have the disciplined life of a boarding school. Many people who could afford it were sending their boys to boarding schools. My brother-in-law, Param, had sent his boys to Lawrence School in Ooty when they were even younger than Shashi. Boarding school was supposed to 'toughen' the boys and make them more independent. Before Shashi had even turned six, he was sent to Montfort School in Yercaud near Salem. Though I had agreed to enroll Shashi in a boarding school, I missed my son terribly and he missed being home. Whenever we called the school office, we heard that Shashi was in the sick room and that his asthma had worsened.

We received long, sad letters from Shashi. Shashi was so much younger than his classmates. Because of his advanced *reading and writing skills, he had been given a double promotion and had been enrolled in a class with boys who were two years older. This made the adjustment with the older boys much more difficult for Shashi. He was a sensitive and creative boy who enjoyed the attention and affection that he got at home from his family. Boarding school didn't seem right for him at all. The experiment with boarding school ended in less than a year, and Shashi was brought back to Bombay. We put him in Campion School which was not far from home. We decided that the girls could start school in Fort Convent, which was close to Campion. It felt good that the family was complete again.*

L to R (front) - M. Subramaniam, R. Ramachandran, B. Srinivasan, Shashi Tharoor
L to R (rear) - Ashok Parameswaran, Cedric Shea, Kailash Advani, Ajith Kumar

With three children at home and all their extracurricular interests keeping us busy, I realized that it was important to learn how to drive so that the car could be used even if the driver was unavailable. I had very sweaty hands and feet throughout my younger years. I was told later that this is a condition called hyperhidrosis. Later, I learned that there were others in the family who had this condition as well. In fact, my feet perspired so much that they would slip out of my chappals. I remember my driving lessons on Chowpatty road near Nariman Point with bare feet on the pedals. I used to hold the steering wheel with a thick towel in my hand! Of course, I had no intention of letting a little problem like this get in the way of my learning. And I still drive with bare feet!

Lily's transformation from a 'simple village girl' to a 'chic city girl' happened in Bombay. Chandran was part of the media scene. He had founded the Advertising Club in the city and knew many interesting, creative people from theatre and from the advertising world. They were mixing with the cream of society. These friends were mavericks and outliers, and they lived with vivacity and verve. Family photographs from that time show Lily in her garden sarees with backcombed hair, large sunglasses and dangling earrings. Gregarious Chandran had friends of all ages, including V. Isvaran, the retired chief Secretary of the Gujarat government, and his wife. So, Lily too learned to bridge generations in her interactions with people. She soon taught herself to overcome the bitter taste of whisky on her tongue in Isvaran's home and learned to have a drink in company. She was also becoming quite used to using English as her primary party language.

Lily was thrilled that Shashi was a voracious reader.

'It was, of course, my mother who'd started me off on the reading habit,' Shashi recalls. "When I was still in diapers, she would read to me from the books on Noddy by Enid Blyton—stories about a nodding wooden doll and his friends in Toyland. My mother jokes that she read them so poorly that I couldn't wait to grab the books from her myself. By the time I was three, I was reading Noddy all by myself.'

Shobha and Smita enjoyed reading for pleasure as well. Lily and the children made frequent trips to the Bombay Gymkhana Library to borrow new books and return the ones they had already read.

Life had a pleasant routine. Shashi was excelling as a student in Campion School and was performing in school plays with the amazing Pearl Padamsee as the school's theatre director. Shobha and Smita were in Fort Convent, which was a sister school to Campion. The children were all remarkable in their academics and extracurricular activities. Both the girls won prizes for their performances on stage at the school's annual talent contests: In Class Two, Shobha transformed into a swan and won a huge applause for her performance of Hans Christian Anderson's story 'The Ugly Duckling'; and kindergartner Smita took the crowd shopping with her confident rendition of the popular English poem 'Let's Go Shopping'.

Shashi was cast as the Artful Dodger in Pearl Padamsee's Campion school production of *Oliver Twist* and became a local celebrity with his outstanding performance. These school productions were so exceptional that they were as good as the productions of professional theatre companies.

Oliver (1968)

Every summer, Lily and Chandran took the children for summer holidays to Kerala. There were some years when Lily's parents would visit them in Bombay. After three years of being away from Kerala during her stay in London, Lily enjoyed the opportunity to be with her family more often. Sadly, Lily's father's last visit to Bombay was for his cancer treatment at the Tata Memorial hospital. He passed away in 1967, leaving Chandran as the responsible elder and the much beloved son-in-law of the Mundarath household. Lily's youngest brother, Jayashankani Amma's youngest son, Mukundan, was only ten years old at the time of his father's death.

The children with both grandmothers in Bombay.

The rhythm of a comfortable life can change when you least expect it. Chandran was about to turn Lily's life upside down.

On 2 February 1968, on the night of their thirteenth wedding anniversary, Chandran suspected that he might be having a heart attack. The next morning, his suspicions were confirmed. Chandran was only thirty-eight years old when he had a massive coronary thrombosis that landed him in the hospital  and kept him in the ICU, battling for his life for six weeks.

If there was a turning point in life for Lily, this was it. Shashi was a month short of twelve. The girls were many years younger. Lily suddenly realized how 'uneducated' and unqualified she was for employment in a big city. It was a sobering moment. While they had lived a comfortable and even an indulgent life thus far because of the many company perquisites for employees, salaries were small and most of it went in just feeding and clothing the family. Chandran was also expected to support his family in the village. There was limited savings in the bank. For the first time in her life, Lily realized how easily she could lose everything that she had become accustomed to.

Despite the gloom, Lily's natural resilience and daily prayers gave her an inner strength while her husband was in the hospital. She realized that she needed to take some of the reins of life in her own hands in the future. She realized that ignorance about day-to-day finance and dependence on the steadiness of one person's employment were a risk. She understood that when times are challenging it is better to seek and find solutions than bemoan life and loss.

Lily immediately enrolled in a correspondence class for a junior college certificate. She made a commitment to herself that she would encourage and assist Chandran in putting away funds to get that necessary 'roof over their head', before his natural generosity made him give away his earnings to others who asked for help.

These qualities of courage and strength are within us all. Lily's inherent curiosity and drive allowed her to not give in to fear. Even if she felt worried or insecure, she always chose to act. Persevering in the face of adversity was her style. 'Get on with it' was one of her many mantras. She had a spiritual courage because of her deep faith in God. She had a bravado because of her upbringing and her life experiences. Lily stayed upbeat and positive for the children, and they in turn helped her persist through the hardship.

7

Honing Talents

Hard Work, Determination and Grit

'You can have anything you want if you want it badly enough.
You can be anything you want to be, do anything you set out to
accomplish, if you hold to that desire with singleness of purpose.'
—Abraham Lincoln

It was easy to become accustomed to the 'stylish' aspects of our
life. Our friends and my husband's colleagues were the founders
of advertising agencies and theatre and media celebrities. We
were used to being invited to all the big events in town. There
were invitations to cocktail parties and book launches. We saw
English plays and classical dance dramas. The 'value' I saw in
these connections and events were that they were opportunities

to allow my children to reach beyond their usual comfort zones. Anything is possible if you set your mind to it is what I believe.

The elegance of the lawn chairs on the green grass of Bombay Gymkhana and the attention of the uniformed bearers of the club made me feel like I was flying, but my upbringing and my Kollengode origins kept me grounded. I knew in my mind that many of these perks in our life were because of the position my husband held and I did not want to take these comforts for granted. I was aware every day that I was married to a heart patient. The realization of that at a young age affected me deeply. I also had my restless, seeking mind. The insecurities brought on by my husband's unstable health kept me both a little dissatisfied and uncomfortable with the stylish lifestyle and the status quo.

Both my husband and I appreciated the opportunity to hone our children's talent and I think we paid more attention to that instead of building a stable bank balance for their future. We were committed to raising the children with an awareness of our family roots and our simple background. Every year after the schools closed, we took Shashi, Shobha and Smita to our tharavad. *Here they were able to bond with their Ammamma, cherriamas, valliamas and mamas in Elevanchery. Since I was the oldest, my youngest sister, Shobana, was only six years older than Shobha, and Mukundan, my youngest brother, was younger than even Shashi. My children became good friends with their uncles and aunts and looked forward to their summer holidays in Mundarath. We also made sure to take them to Chittlamchery to meet my husband's side of the family. In these yearly visits, the children practised their Malayalam, experienced the Kerala customs and cuisine, and participated in festivals and other family pastimes. They bathed in the pozha, watched murukku and kondatam and nayyu preparation at home—and enjoyed other village-life experiences that were impossible to find in the city. I remember my husband telling the children, 'You must be able to eat as comfortably with your fingers on the banana leaf in Kerala as you do with your fork and knife at the club.' He was teaching them the importance of being comfortable in both their worlds. Today, I'm proud of the children for living their lives as global citizens. They are as comfortable in Elevanchery as they are in any big city in the world. And my grandchildren, too, look forward to their visits to India and settle in easily when they are here.*

My husband was always volunteering and getting involved in activities outside his work. He never denied help to anyone who sought it. He helped set up the Advertising Club in Bombay with his friend Sylvie DaCunha and together they spread the word about creative networking. I was busy in my Films Division career and was once invited by music director, P. Bhaskaran, to audition for a playback-singing opportunity. I became over confident in the studio and sang a song at a much higher note than I needed to and my voice cracked. Perhaps I had compensated for my nervousness. It was definitely a lesson I learned. Grand opportunities don't come all that often and we must make the most of it with practice and effort. I heard a saying later in America: 'failure to prepare is preparing to fail.' It is definitely an important life lesson.

Shobha started Bharatanatyam classes as an afterschool activity in Fort Convent with a teacher called Padmini (who would soon become a famous Bollywood star) and my chatterbox,

Smita, kept us all entertained by her questions and riddles. It was a magical time but once again change was around the corner. It seemed that the opportunity to live in Calcutta, an opportunity that I missed right after my marriage when we left for London instead, was now about to happen. Our beautiful Bombay days were coming to an end.

Calcutta was a city very different from Bombay. It seemed like the British life and habits still lingered in the city. Even the colonial buildings in Calcutta gave it a different feel. Both sides of Park Street were dotted with English-style pubs and restaurants. Baked beans and chicken on toast, delectable pastries and English tea were the popular items on the menu at Flury's—the famous patisserie on Park Street—while shrimp cocktails and chicken Kiev were the signature dishes at Mocambo! It was a city where commerce slowed in the afternoons when the Bengali *babus* took their siesta. After the busy pace and vibrant energy of Bombay, it felt like time stood still in Calcutta. But Lily loved the pace of the city, the welcoming people, and the respectful, helpful staff that she was able to hire. She said that Calcutta was her favourite of all the cities that she had made a home in.

They moved to Calcutta in January 1969, and started the first few months of their life in the city in a large, colonial-style mansion which had been vacated by the recently departed editor. Lily found the large house difficult to manage and was delighted when they moved into a posh new flat in the high-walled twin tower building complex called Minto Park.

Minto Park was in the Alipore area where other executives of multinational companies were also allotted flats. They began a new and exciting phase of their lives. Desmond Doig, the writer, painter, photographer, expeditioner and editor of *Junior Statesman*, lived in one of the towers of Minto Park as well. He hosted a number of celebrities in his flat while they were there, including the American actress, Shirley MacLaine, and the Hindi film heartthrob of the time, Dev Anand. Desmond used to dabble as unofficial landscaper of the beautiful Minto Park gardens in his spare time, and the glorious blooms of the giant dahlias that he personally tended to always won the first prize at the Calcutta Annual Flower Show.

It was a wonderful, colourful life, and it was a life of opportunity and visibility.

One of the city's highlights each year was the Statesman Vintage Car Rally that had begun as an annual festival in 1968. As the seat of the British Empire for 139 years, Calcutta (now Kolkata) had inherited a fondness for the British way of life, perhaps more than any other city in India. As Chandran was a top executive in the newspaper, his family had front-row access to this and other media-covered events. British-era vehicles were paraded down the streets with pomp and festivity. Lily and the girls would be at the starting point, dressed to the nines on the cold January morning to see a dignitary wave off the first classic automobile. It was a day of celebration. It was a day like no other.

Life in Calcutta for Lily was very easy as she had full-time staff support at home, a driver to take them everywhere,

Saturday Club Membership and many other indulgences. Shobha and Smita got admission in the well-reputed all girls' Catholic school, Loreto House, on Middleton Row near Park Street and were excelling in their classes. Shashi began his stint at St Xavier's Collegiate School by the time he was a teenager and had already established himself as the academic star of the class. But Lily was not one to sink into an easy existence. She needed challenges to overcome, or excitement to shake up the day's routine. In 1971, Lily joined a group of ladies, many of whom she didn't know, and took a trip without her husband to London. It was an adventure. She came back with news of European fashion and gifts of trendy stretch pants and stylish tunics for the girls and a psychedelic shimmery shirt for Shashi. Her sartorial tastes were always outside the traditional box. She also brought home the number-one hit single of that year, 'Chirpy Chirpy Cheep Cheep'. With its catchy refrain of 'Where's your mama gone? Where's your papa gone', the song by the Scottish band, Middle of the Road, was a family favourite for many years.

Lily subscribed to the notion that 'intelligence without ambition is like a bird without wings'. She knew that her children had the potential to shine beyond school. They had proven themselves in Bombay, and she was not going to let their inertia or reticence get in the way of similar accolades in Calcutta. She was determined to get the children recognized for their talents in this new city as well. She met Aditi Shyam, who worked in public relations at ITC, at a social event soon after their transfer to Calcutta, and learnt that Aditi was the host of a children's programme on All India Radio. Without reservation or hesitation, Lily lauded the talents of her three children to Aditi. All three of her children were soon on air!

As a top executive in the city's leading newspaper, Chandran was able to offer the children many opportunities to attend cultural events and Lily was sure to urge them to make use of it. They had front-row seats to concerts (Cliff Richards when he had a concert tour in India) and scholarly lectures at the Birla Planetarium. They were invited to film retrospectives at the USIS and the British Council, had tickets to tennis tournaments with nationally ranked players at local clubs and prized seats to Test cricket matches in the Eden Gardens. Lily recognized that it was a life of privilege. But if there was learning and growth from each encounter or opportunity, then there was significance in that reward.

Shashi had already proven himself as a writer in Bombay. His first short story, 'Henry's Last Battle', was published in the *Bharat Jyoti*, the Sunday edition of the Free Press Journal when he was only ten. When he wrote his first novel, *Operation Bellows*, a year later, he sent it to *JS* and was delighted when they published it over six instalments as a serialized book.* Shashi soon became a frequent contributor to the magazine. The iconic *JS* was the launching pad for so

---

* 'Henry's Last Battle' was published in the *Bharat Jyoti*, the Sunday edition of the Free Press Journal in January 1967, and *Operation Bellows* was published in the *Junior Statesman* over six installments as a serialized book in 1967.

many well-regarded writers and journalists today. Shobha and Smita embraced theatre, debate and elocution, and won local and state competitions in Elocution. Lily started Rabindra Sangeet lessons so she could better understand the cultural fibre of the city that she had grown to love.

By then, Lily had become quite a well-respected cook and her pickles were in demand among her friends. So, she decided to join the Calcutta Canning Centre and learn to bottle and jar her culinary creations for gifting and perhaps even for sale. She sent out her recipes and 'household hints' to the *Eve's Weekly* and *Femina* magazines that she'd read regularly, and was pleased to see her name and writing soon in print on the pages of the same magazines. Since she was not working outside the home, Lily also joined Mother Teresa's Missionaries of Charity on A.J.C. Bose Road and offered whatever help she could with time or resources. Shashi remembers that during his early years at the United Nations, when his mother visited him in Geneva, she made him take her to homes in Switzerland where children, who had been adopted from Shishu Bhavan, now resided. Lily would reassure herself that the adoptees from Calcutta were happy and well looked after, and, when she returned to Calcutta, she would inform Mother Teresa's sisters that all was well.

Meanwhile, Chandran, true to his social work ethic, had started the Bengal/Kerala Cultural Society and was busy with committee meetings and cultural events, sharing ideas and bringing people together. He was often the go-to person for the newcomers in the city.

Life was busy and fulfilling. Shashi recalls that his parents never forgot where they came from, and the bedroom that was allotted to him had to be regularly shared with someone who came from the village to the city for job training and a leg up in life. Since they had a spacious living room, Lily and Chandran's Minto Park flat saw many Durga Pujo, Diwali and Onam celebrations and their living room was often a launching pad and salon for singers like Usha Uthup and K.J. Yesudas and celebrities like the 'human computer' Shakuntala Devi. The children grew up in an atmosphere of talent and community.

Will's Filter 'Made for Each Other' Contest, 1972

Calcutta was a politically minded place and the city had frequent unrest and agitation. There was an influx of refugees from East Bengal who had made a home in the city after the Bangladesh Liberation War. The poverty in some parts of Calcutta was quite acute and visible. Some residents felt that the state's resources were diminished by the Bangladeshi refugees. Others felt that not enough was being done to address refugees' needs. There were frequent strikes, and many of the city's unemployed population took to the streets with demands for adequate food, affordable public transport, fair wages and accommodation. Activists demanded peasant rights and added their voice to the cries of the agitators. Protestors were usually led by the Left-leaning political parties and all this disquiet meant frequent city bandhs. Though the essence of the political demands sprung from a compassionate place and was borne from a desire to uproot an unresponsive government, more dangerous fringe elements mushroomed in the city. The far-Left Communist rebels who were part of the Naxalite movement created problems and serious disturbances to life in the city. These movements gave Calcutta and its people a distinct character: politically aware and culturally vibrant, but often a place where progress seemed impossible for its youth. The city became synonymous with stagnation in many people's minds.

Calcutta monsoons were relentless and the city's streets were frequently clogged and affected by floods. But even the excessive rain didn't stop Lily in her tracks! If she promised the children a movie outing, and their car stalled in the water-logged streets, she would exit the car, lift up her sari and wade with them to their promised outing! A 'fearless (perhaps foolish) risk-taker' is how Chandran referred to her with fondness.

Lily questioned the status quo of a routine existence. 'I have my own way of functioning,' she would say proudly to friends who suggested that she was always busy. She encouraged the children to seize every minute in the day and make the most of every opportunity that came their way. If schools were closed, there were other things that could be done with their free time. In the words of the American engineer Harrington Emerson: 'Without ambition one starts nothing. Without work one finishes nothing. The prize will not be sent to you. You have to win it.'* These lines echoed constantly in Lily's mind. She was driven and she was ambitious. She told herself that in order to get the best out of every situation, she needed to set goals and work towards them. She called it 'a focus in life'.

---

* These words are often wrongly attributed to poet Ralph Waldo Emerson. Chris Hanlon, 'On Fake Emerson Quotes', Avidly (27 August 2019), online.

8

The School of Life

'Nothing we learn in this world is ever wasted.'

—Eleanor Roosevelt

Shashi was always a brilliant student. I remember, he would get top marks in all the subjects, and so, at prize distribution ceremonies, the teachers would call his name for every subject and he would have to leave his seat repeatedly to go to the stage. He would get the General Proficiency prize as well for the top rank in class and we would bring home a tall stack of books as a reward each year. This is a memory imprinted in my mind. The girls would accompany us to the award ceremony. They were so proud of their Etta. Shashi was only fifteen when he took the Senior Cambridge exams and earned five points in his exams. He stood first in school even in Lower Hindi which was his most challenging subject. When I look at him today and see how busy he is, I feel I may have made him feel too responsible from an early age because of my own insecurities.

I grew up at a time when we expected our sons to be our emotional and financial support. Even today, Shashi is always working. I teasingly call him 'a machine', but I feel I am responsible and have influenced this workaholic lifestyle. I think my children are all too serious. I had never let them waste time when they were children. After all these years, I do wonder if I made a mistake in the way I influenced their focus in life.

My husband wanted Shashi to study in the best college and in a city in which regular strikes and bandhs didn't delay the exams. However, there is one decision of ours that I am proud of. Shashi said he wanted to study History in college. Many friends pointed out that studying this subject would not easily lead to a job. They said that the subject would be a waste of Shashi's talent and brilliance. He was so clever and could pursue any field. At a time when children were being pushed towards medicine and engineering, I'm glad that we had the confidence to encourage Shashi to study the subject that interested him. Shashi has now proven to be an example of someone who continued to excel in his studies and his work by following his dreams. He was not even sixteen when we heard the news that Shashi had been accepted to the prestigious St Stephen's College in New Delhi.

Our family changed when Shashi left home in 1972. Shobha was barely twelve and Smita was only ten. We had just survived a very difficult six months as Smita had contracted bacterial meningitis and had only recently recovered. My brave Swattu had to be treated with sixty steroid injections and a special diet to build up her strength. She was asthmatic like her brother and we were always worried about her health.

After Shashi left for college, I turned my full attention back to my daughters. The girls were only twenty-one months apart and to me they were like twins even if their personalities were different. They still complain about how I dressed them in identical clothes for a long time. Both the girls had distinguished themselves in school. They represented Loreto in local and state elocution contests and brought home many prizes. Shobha was doing well in both science and humanities subjects. She joined the Leadership Training Service and was busy with community projects on the weekends and holidays. The principal at Loreto House said it was necessary to keep Smita back a year because she had missed more than six months of classes because of her illness. Smita was not happy about repeating a class but we felt that it would be less of a physical strain for her. There were many Loreto girls living in Minto Park and Smita had many friends to play with every day.

I visited Shashi in Delhi once or twice when he was at Stephen's. Shashi had made a name for himself in Delhi University. He had become popular at college festivals (where he and Ramu Damodaran won all the debate, dramatics and quiz competitions), in theatre, and later by winning the elections for student president of the University. He used to come home to Calcutta during the holidays and sometimes he brought his friends as well to stay with us. Shashi had grown taller in college and looked like a man now with long sideburns and a different sartorial style. Shobha once remarked that many of the senior *students in her school were friendly with her even though she was only in the sixth standard. She thought it was probably because they wanted to meet her illustrious brother. In 1976, Shashi was awarded the prestigious Rajika Kriplani Memorial Award for young journalists. My husband was the most excited about this.*

Meanwhile, though the girls' interests were more toward books than clothes, I tried to groom them to be fashionable so they could participate and win beauty pageants. The 'Tharoor Sisters' got a lot of attention in those days at all the public events that we would attend. I thought that with their confidence, ability to speak well and good looks, they would be 'discovered' and their futures would always be secure. I still feel that being a good student did not have to be at the expense of other achievements. My girls didn't fully agree with me as they were not interested in modeling and films but wanted to be known as debaters and writers like their brother. They were too bookish!

Despite the ongoing political turbulence in Calcutta, including the Emergency which caused most newspaper outlets to be susceptible to scrutiny and monitoring, Lily and Chandran's time in the city were some of the best years of their working life. They had the 'full life' that Lily desired, and the comfort of many close and dear friends for company. Shobha finished her ICSE exams, and, emboldened by an excellent school production of *The Merchant of Venice* in tenth grade, she joined a local theatre group. She also won a Nivea Crème-sponsored beauty contest (judged by the newly crowned Miss India, Nafisa Ali), played Juliet in a production of Romeo and Juliet at the British Council, and took on a few modeling gigs to pay for her French classes at the Alliance française. She started her plus II in Loreto College and thought ahead about college applications for her Bachelor's degree. She and Smita also participated in fashion shows at Saturday Club. There were many interesting events happening in the city. Smita was invited to audition for a part in the film *36 Chowringhee Lane* with Jennifer Kapoor. Aparna Sen, the director, was casting for the role of a young student. Unfortunately, Smita's convent-informed English accent didn't work out for the role of a traditional Bengali girl. But Smita took the disappointment in her usual stride. She was busy and happy, and a confident leader. Soon, she was elected the vice-captain of Gandhi House in school.

When Shashi was in the USA on a fellowship pursuing a doctorate at the Fletcher School of Law and Diplomacy, he encouraged Shobha to apply to colleges in America for her undergraduate studies. He thought that with her dual interest in Biology and Literature, she might do well in the multi-subject Liberal Arts curriculum in America rather than be limited by the specificity of one honours subject as was expected at Loreto College. Chandran had always said that he would support his daughters to follow their dreams just like he had their brother, but Shobha knew that it was imperative that she receive financial assistance if she was to be able to afford to study abroad. She decided to apply for admission only if it offered a full scholarship and began studying in earnest for the SATs by learning new words each day from *Reader's Digest* magazines.

In 1977, when he was only twenty-one years old, Shashi returned from Boston and announced that he wished to be married to Tillottama Mukherjee (Minu) whom he had met in Delhi when he was at St. Stephen's and she was a graduate student at Hindu College.

For the first time in her life, Lily felt panicked and terrified for the future. Chandran was not of the most robust physical health and she felt vulnerable thinking of the years ahead. She knew that it was Chandran's joyful nature and community spirit that kept him engaged in many activities, not his good health. Like many women of her generation, Lily had imagined that her son would be her asset and strength for the future. She had hoped that he would be able to assist her when it was time to 'settle' her daughters in marriage. Shashi's announcement to marry so young was another turning point in her life.

Lily with Shobha & Smita, August 1977

In 1978, Shobha took the SATs and applied to universities in America for undergraduate studies. She thought that she would be going to the country where her brother resided, but Shashi was married by then. He had accelerated his studies, completed his PhD at the age of twenty-two and received a job offer with the United Nations in Geneva, Switzerland. If she was to travel and live in America, it would have to be without her brother's presence or support in the country.

In 1979, the pageant organizers of the Femina Miss India contest noticed Shobha and Smita at the Saturday Club where they were dining with their parents.

Though the nationwide contest trials had concluded, the organizers invited the girls to submit applications for the regional contest in Calcutta. Lily was the most excited, and encouraged her less than enthusiastic daughters. She had read enough about the many confident young women who had won in the previous years and gone on to build successful film careers.

In March 1979, Shobha was crowned Miss Calcutta and Smita won the first runner-up title. The girls' photographs were splashed in all the Calcutta dailies the next day. Both Shobha and Smita would be going to Bombay for the Miss India title. With her long tresses, slender build and height, Smita was selected as the first runner-up of Miss India in Bombay. Swaroop Sampat took the Miss India title that year. Lily hoped that the girls would be catapulted into a glamorous world. But, a few weeks later, a full scholarship offer for Shobha came as a telegram from Elmira College in New

York. An i20 visa offer followed. Smita, meanwhile, decided that she wanted a change of place and the opportunity to make up for the year that she had lost because of her illness and left for Sophia College, Ajmer. Shobha too left for New York within a few weeks. Suddenly, the house was empty. The glamour and fame that Lily sought for her girls was not to be. Lily braced herself for the change.

In February 1980, Lily and Chandran visited Shashi in his new flat in Geneva. It was their first holiday together abroad after they had returned to India from England. For their 25th wedding anniversary, Shashi and Minu had gifted them 'Round the World' air tickets so they could stop by in New York first and visit Shobha in Elmira College. It had been more than six months since they had seen her. It was in Geneva that Chandran told his son that he was seriously considering leaving *The Statesman* and accepting an invitation to work for the *Reader's Digest*. He had been offered this job before but had always turned it down as long as his own brother was its chief executive.

Back in Calcutta, after their holiday, Lily made the decision that, despite her lack of degrees, she would apply for a job so she wouldn't feel the painful absence of her children. She submitted an application to a company called Avid Limited that produced paper products and was pleasantly surprised when she was offered a position as the accounts executive for the princely salary of Rs 1,000 a month. But, before she could consider accepting the job, Chandran announced to Lily that he had decided to end his many years at *The Statesman*, and would soon be joining the *Reader's Digest* as director of advertising. They would be moving back to Bombay. By the end of 1980, Chandran and Lily had left Calcutta and moved back to Bombay for their second stint in the city. This time, it was to Malabar Hill in South Mumbai.

Your choices, your actions and your experiences are your best teacher. Lily had been a conductor of her children's life experiences but she was a student of life as well. She had lived long enough to know that everyone reaches at least one crossroad in their life and often not by their own choice. Crossroads may be scary but she was determined to think of them as a place of opportunity, and never overthink any of her decisions. It was part of the courage with which she had approached everything in life.

9

Closed Doors. Open Windows

'If you're brave enough to say goodbye, life will reward you with a new hello.'

—Paulo Coelho

We were in Bombay for only seven years but it was a time of many important events in our life. I decided that I was going to commit to daily exercise like my husband had for many years and walked every day from our home 'Sea Belle', on Napean Sea Road, to the Mahalakshmi Temple on Bhulabhai Desai Marg. It was about 2 kilometres each way but I was happy to walk with a purpose of visiting the temple. I would recite my prayers as I walked back.

I had started reading more English books at that time, but I also enjoyed the magazines that came home every week as it gave me a chance to see how people lived and how their thoughts were changing. Young people had so many ideas that seemed new or unusual to me. Life had changed so much since I was young like them. I read in these magazines that the new generation felt the frustrations of being born without their choice; youngsters said that they were unhappy for not being able to choose their parents; they even wrote that they did not get along or 'connect' with their parents and family members; when anything went wrong with their life or with their expectations, they seemed to blame others. I felt like reminding them that a large part of their life's journey was predetermined from their previous birth. This life is their karma, and they are meant to do better by learning from their past life's mistakes. I believe that the parents are also decided by the creator, as children and their parents were connected in some way in an earlier birth. My life and my readings give me strength in these convictions. I have read a few books on reincarnation as well, which confirms my thoughts. I often wonder how I had been born in a village and yet had a different exposure than my siblings. Maybe this life of mine was destined to happen and I was meant to live like this. I must have brought the good and bad with me from a previous birth. It was up to me to make the very best of this life. When I hear about so many broken homes and read articles about unhappy people everywhere, I hope that an institution like marriage endures. I know that all of us need an anchor in life and someone to share our thoughts and dreams. It can be a woman with a woman, or a man with a man also, but companionship is necessary for everyone. We must cherish the people in our life. If modern life continues like this with fractured homes and selfish thinking, robots will soon take over and provide company to single people. Then only machines will look after us, understand us and answer our needs.

We reconnected with our old friends and resumed a part of our old life in Bombay after we settled in Sea Belle. The children kept in touch regularly with newsy letters. As phone calls were prohibitively expensive, we limited our international calls. In May 1981, Shashi and Minu moved to Singapore where Shashi was posted as the Head of Mission at the UNHCR in Singapore and was in charge of helping with the boat people crisis of displaced Vietnamese after the Vietnam War. He was only twenty-five! We were extremely proud of him.

My life has always been full of coincidences and connections. When we lived in Kasturi Building with my husband in charge of the Bombay office, Mr Taroon Kumar Bhaduri was in a cubicle in the same office as the Statesman's *Bombay correspondent. This was of course many years before his daughter, Jaya, had become a famous actress. Many years later, in 1982, my husband was in the ICU of Breach Candy Hospital, recovering from his second major heart attack and in the next room in the ICU was Jaya Bhaduri's husband, Amitabh Bachchan, who was recovering from a serious injury that happened during a film shooting. Taroon Kumar Bhaduri came to visit his son-in-law in the ICU so we were able to meet him once again after all these years. But this time the circumstances were different and the 'power structure' had changed.*

Lily and Chandran's second stint in Bombay was a time of both trials and celebrations. Each year brought news and activity that was beyond the mundane into their lives. Smita was married in 1982, but stayed back in Ajmer to finish her college degree. Chandran was not in good health at the time of Smita's marriage. He had ongoing angina pains and was confined to bed for a large part of the marriage ceremony. It worried everyone. Shashi contacted cardiologist friends in Singapore with his father's medical reports and they said that a by-pass and open-heart surgery was absolutely necessary. In March 1983, Shashi made all the financial arrangements for his father's treatment at the Cleveland Clinic in the USA where Dr Floyd Loop had perfected the catheterization process in heart surgery. Shashi flew to Bombay and travelled with his father from India to America for the procedure. A professor friend was kind enough to drive Shobha to be with her brother and father in Cleveland, Ohio, during the surgery. Lily, Jayashankini and Smita prayed from afar in India.

Despite extensive damage to the heart wall because of his first serious heart attack, Chandran's open-heart surgery of a single by-pass, a balloon angioplasty and an aortic aneurysm repair was deemed a success. Dr Floyd Loop, who performed the surgery, announced that Chandran's heart was 'as good as new'! Once again, a catastrophe in their collective lives seemed to have been averted.

The same year saw some health issues for Lily, and she had to have surgery as well. Smita had moved by then to London to join her husband before their first anniversary so Lily was on her own during her surgery. Meanwhile, Shobha decided to quit the doctoral programme at Syracuse. At twenty-two, she felt unfocused and ill-prepared to spend the many years of scholarship required in graduate school for a PhD. She was also quite homesick by then and intended to return to India with a Master's degree. But her year-long friendship with Raj Srinivasan had developed into something else and, when he left Syracuse to work in California, the time apart confirmed their love. Raj promised the homesick Shobha that India was only a plane ride away. A few months later, in October of the same year, Shobha came home to get married.

The next year brought with it another blessing. In 1984, Minu and Shashi became parents of twin boys, and Lily and Chandran were grandparents for the first time. Lily and Chandran awaited their grandsons' visit to India with mounting excitement. When they were all finally together in Bombay, a puja and the traditional 'chorunnu' (annaprasan) was performed in the Kochu Guruvayoor Temple in Matunga as Lily wanted.

Grandparenthood continued. In 1985, Shobha gave birth to a daughter and Lily was thrilled to have a little girl in the family this time who would keep up the matrilineal line. Shobha brought Ragini home to Bombay for two months when she was less than three months old and it was a time of endless joy for everyone. Lily set up a *thottil* in her bedroom with a sari and fully immersed herself in the pleasure of having a baby at home. Chandran was thrilled as well to have the profound happiness of a cooing, gurgling infant with them. They were heartbroken when their 'precious' had to board the plane back to California with her mother. Lily was determined that visits abroad would have to happen: she needed to see her granddaughter before long.

The arrival of their grandchildren changed Lily and Chandran's travel and life routine. They made a pact to take turns visiting America every year if they couldn't afford to make the trip together. Whenever Lily was in America, her mother would come to Bombay to be of help and company to Chandran.

But, once again, change was waiting around the corner. Chandran was no longer in the frame of mind and body to continue the demanding life expected of an advertising professional in fast-paced Bombay. Chandran's former colleague at *The Statesman,* Bikram Singh, suggested to Chandran that he should move to New Delhi and join him in a new business venture. As Chandran pondered the possibility of entrepreneurship, he received a job offer from the Patriot group of papers. The work seemed interesting and, in 1987, he accepted the job and made the decision to move to the nation's capital. They had been in Bombay for seven years during his second posting!

Both in her travels abroad and in her life at home, Lily displayed confidence and independence. Smita remembers that when her mother couldn't open the lid of a jar, she would not wait for assistance or the stronger wrist of another person, but would instead uncap the jar by opening its lid using the door jamb! She was now interested in using that spirit to further a different goal. Despite the empty house, there was some calm in Lily's otherwise turbulent mind because her children were all 'settled' with life partners of their choice. Her goal now was to establish a 'home of her own', and she was determined. This progressive thinking was a consistent part of Lily's 'focus'. She had the restlessness of a 'doer' and was always striving to achieve a goal. Ambitious people push forward and are determined to succeed. They don't give up. They work hard, persevere and are dedicated to what they want out of their life.

10

Travels and Trials

'You have to dream before your dreams can come true.'
—A.P.J. Abdul Kalam

Life in Delhi as fifty-year-olds was different. We were not the young and dynamic couple that we had been in Bombay and Calcutta. My husband was no longer an executive with all the perks and support of a big company. Everything seemed less certain and our lifestyles had changed. But it didn't bother me too much. In Delhi too we easily connected with old and new friends and there were a lot of people with Kerala connections who wanted to be in our lives. We continued to have a busy social life. Here too we had parties and card sessions on weekends as my husband found a group of friends to play '56' with him in every city we lived.

New Delhi was different from all the cities we had lived in before. It was much more organized with traffic more orderly. The city had more of a Hindi and North Indian culture, but my husband and I spoke our own version of Hindi—even if our vocabulary was poor and the grammar was incorrect—so we managed. Since we both enjoyed new experiences and meeting new people (after all we are both Sagittarians), we were able to settle down easily in the nation's capital. We lived in the Greater Kailash area which was more down to earth and middle class. Once I found the markets I needed to shop in, and a temple close by for my regular visits, I was happy. We became close friends with our neighbours and reconnected with a few old friends from Calcutta who were now posted in Delhi.

It was exciting to live in a place so full of ancient history and old structures. We could show visitors from Kerala the Red Fort and Purana Quila and Qutub Minar—structures that they had only studied about in their history books. There was also Connaught Place which was a little like Colaba in Bombay with all the cafes and restaurants and shops. And there was Lodhi Gardens which was beautiful just like Hanging Gardens near our old home in Bombay. Delhi had plenty of things to offer: every year, there were book festivals in Pragati Maidan and craft fairs and mango festivals in Surajkund. If you had a car and a driver, which we did, going out for interesting events in the city was not difficult. In 1991, I remember, we went to Pragati Maidan to pick up Shashi's Commonwealth Writers' Prize for The Great Indian Novel. *The writer Anita Desai gave the award to my husband as Shashi could not come from New York to collect his prize.*

Since the children's needs were no longer something to worry about, I could think about our own need to build a roof over our head. Going home to live in the tharavad *permanently was not something either of us wanted to do. We had lived outside of Kerala for too long. We had put some savings away and, adding some money from my husband's provident fund, we were able to buy a two-bedroom flat in a building that was being constructed in Patparganj. This was an industrial area close to the Uttar Pradesh border that was an 'up and coming' place, and we thought that if we did not want to live in North India after our retirement, we could later sell the flat for profit and buy or build elsewhere. So, we bought the flat but continued to live in the place we had rented in Greater Kailash. GK was a more convenient location for my husband to meet people and clients for his work.*

In a few years, Shashi also decided that he wanted to invest in property in Delhi so he and Minu bought a flat on a nice residential street in GK2. He told us that we should move into his property and not waste our savings on rent. We soon become caretakers of his flat in GK2. Shashi was at the UN head office by then and they were living in New York City with their boys.

We decided to rent out the Patparganj flat once we took possession of it. But, despite my suggestion that we should only rent to a known person who had come recommended by a friend, my husband rented the flat to a lady who answered our ad in the paper. She had an unemployed husband and an unstable job. Every month, this lady would come home and plea for an extension on the rent payment. Soon the rents stopped coming altogether. All this caused tension for my husband and annoyed me.. It probably affected his health as well. I told my husband that we should buy a plot of land in Bangalore where we could build a flat after we sold the property in Patparganj. After so many years of living outside of Kerala, I wanted us to live somewhere in a city and not in a small town.

Smita had her first child in 1990 and we went with great excitement to meet our new grandson. Both my husband and I enjoyed travelling to London as it was a place familiar to us. On one of the trips that he made on his own, my husband took Smita down memory lane. They went to all the previous flats he had occupied and we had lived in together after marriage. He showed her the India Club on the Strand where he had performed before India's first High Commissioner to the UK, V.K. Krishna Menon. The performance was an original satirical Ottamthullal that my husband had composed and written himself. Many years later, to raise the profile of the India Club, Smita hosted a reception and dinner with speeches followed by the unveiling of four historic photographs that included her father. It was a nostalgic tribute to an institution which her father had co-founded. Recently, when the same India Club, which had been that home away from home and a meeting place for people from the subcontinent since the Fifties, came under the threat of developers who wished to demolish and renovate the historic building, Smita joined the efforts and worked hard to prevent changes to the Club.

On his visit to London, my husband showed her the newspaper offices on Fleet Street as well. Later when I visited London, Smita took me to Trinity Court where I had lived when

Shashi was a baby. My husband and I took turns travelling abroad as it was easier managing the cost of one airfare and only one of us was away from India at a time. With all three children in foreign places, we kept our passports in good use.

On the trips to America, we had to fly to both coasts as Shashi was in New York and Shobha was in California. I enjoyed going to New York city where I could walk around on my own and be useful to Shashi and Minu. I liked the energy and busy life of the city. I used to drop off the dry cleaning for them, walk to the library and run other errands in New York. In Shobha's house, it was different. She lived in the suburbs. To me, San Jose seemed like a village in comparison to the big cities in India and I needed to depend on Shobha to go anywhere. She had to use the car for everything. But I still liked visiting them as my precious and only granddaughter was in San Jose and that made the visit so much more enjoyable. The boys were all very different and they had less time for me and my ideas.

Lily brought her curiosity, drive and ambition with her on those visits to her children and grandchildren. She poured her seeking, driving spirit into her granddaughter, 'Ragini baby', who was particularly interested in what her grandmother had to say. Lily was not a very traditional grandmother. She was not one who did art projects with the grandchildren or taught them science. Lily cooked occasionally, but cooking was never her sole interest and she did not have the patience or inclination to perfect a dish or be tidy in its preparation. But she shared other skills in the kitchen: she didn't let a vegetable go to waste in the fridge; many recipes were concocted with stalks and stems and she turned lemons from the garden into delectable pickles that could be bottled and shared. Despite her fluency in English, Lily tried to speak to her grandchildren in Malayalam as she always thought it was important to know multiple languages. She even tried to teach them bhajans and prayers. But her teaching style was laidback and best received by a child with an open mind and a listening nature.

Lily would go for walks in the neighborhood and pick up the free city newspapers stacked outside store fronts to bring back and share. She would point out contests to enter, and highlight events for her granddaughter's participation. On one visit, at her grandmother's insistence, Ragini wrote a short essay for Mother's Day and won the first prize of four tickets to a water theme park by entering a contest that was announced in the community paper. On another visit, Lily thumbed through the popular *American Girl* magazine, and noticed that it had paper dolls of real-life girls whose ancestors came from other countries. Lily realized that they had yet to feature an Indian American, and told her granddaughter that this ought to be accomplished. Ragini dutifully wrote to the magazine and, to her delight, the magazine asked for additional information. Lily and Chandran gathered the requisite photos and stories about Ragini's foremothers. The result was a paper pop-out version of Ragini with the accompanying text: 'Meet Ragini Srinivasan—and some of the remarkable women in her family. Ten-year-old Ragini lives in San Jose, California.

She can trace her family back 100 years, to her great-great-grandmother who lived in India!"*

All of this was quintessentially Lily. She embarked on every journey with an open mind and observed her surroundings with a sharp eye, seeking opportunities. Over the years, once she was comfortable using the Internet, she was known to search for addresses of authors whose books she had enjoyed, and she unabashedly emailed them her comments, compliments, informal reviews and even questions. Sometimes these authors would write back. They might even become friends. Audacity was part of Lily's DNA and it was difficult to not come under the spell of her infectious courage and drive. Years later, she would pat her children on their back when their names appeared in print by saying, 'Good to get publicity. It makes you more energetic.' She said she used to feel that rush of energy when she was broadcasting for All India Radio and recording Malayalam advertisements.

In 1992, when Chandran and Lily were both visiting Smita in London during the birth of her second son, Chandran had another heart attack. It was a mild one, but he spent a few days in the hospital. The insensitive doctors there advised him to go back home and 'put his affairs in order'. This was a big blow to Chandran's naturally ebullient spirit that had him presuming that the by-pass

---

* Ragini was featured in the August/September 1995 issue of *American Girl* magazine. She was the eighteenth paper doll in the series.

surgery done nine years ago in America had continued to remain effective. It was a difficult realization for Lily as well. In her heart, she braced for another change. Shashi called his father and asked him to hang up his boots. Chandran and Lily began the process of winding up their Delhi life and made plans to go together to America to spend several months with Shobha and her family.

In March 1993, they arrived in San Jose, CA. No one knew at the time but it was Chandran's last visit to America. On that trip, they travelled to other cities and met old friends. It was a swan song for Chandran. While they were in San Jose with Shobha and Raj, both Shashi and Smita came for the Vishu celebration, bringing their children with them.

Family portrait (includes children and grandchildren) taken on Chandran's last visit to California

But, despite the happy times spent together, there was a worry in everyone's mind. Chandran's angina pains were more frequent. He tired easily as well. And then, in June, he caught chicken pox. In August 1993, Lily and Chandran went back to India to make plans for their retired life. The flat in Patparganj remained locked up in a rent impasse with a tenant who refused to vacate and refused to pay rent. The land in Bangalore had been sold to a developer who also reneged on the promise of a proper flat in the building he developed. They had essentially been allotted a large room. It was also far away from the heart of the city and Lily was increasingly feeling that she needed to be closer to where her mother and other family lived.

They went back to Lily's tharavad, where Chandran could rest in a place of love and regard while Lily looked for a flat to rent in Coimbatore, the city closest to her mother's home in Kerala. There was a lorry strike at the time and their furniture and other personal belongings that had been shipped from Delhi lay in limbo in a godown in Bangalore. In the midst of other chaos, Lily rushed to Bangalore to sort things out and made sure that their belongings were finally on the way to Coimbatore.

Two weeks after moving into Raheja Apartments on Avinashi Road in Coimbatore, Chandran woke up one morning, had his bath, said his prayers and, sitting down on his bed, breathed his last. He was only sixty-three years old. It was not a massive heart attack. It was a gentle cardiac arrest. His heart was too tired to keep on going. Lily's mother was in Coimbatore visiting and helping out at the time. She was scheduled to depart later that morning so Lily's brother, Narayan Unni, had come from Elevanchery to take his mother back home. Lily was blessed, therefore, to have her mother and her brother at home when Chandran took his last breath. Chandran had always been Jayashankini Amma's favourite. She was meant to be there when he left them all.

How would it be from now on for Lily who had been preparing for this loss for such a long time? She was only fifty-seven years old. Lily's faith gave her strength and her goals gave her purpose. How does a strong woman face one of the largest trials of her life? She decides to face her fears head on. She decides not to run away from the challenges by surrendering them to someone else to solve.

11

On Her Own

'However bad life may seem, there is always something you can do, and succeed at. While there's life, there's hope.'
—Stephen Hawking

Shashi, Shobha and Smita came from different parts of the world to say goodbye to their daddy. They stayed with me for a few weeks but I knew they would need to return to their families soon, and I would need to manage life on my own. I was determined to be independent. Shashi had his own struggles and personal demands in life. And my girls were also busy with their young children and their husbands. It was up to me how I wanted to live my life in the future. I told myself that I would not underestimate myself or overestimate my problems. And I had my Swami to give me strength. Sathya Sai Baba had come into my life at the right time; only a few years earlier when I had not even been looking for him, but it was he who I turned to most often for comfort. Whatever Swami decides, that is what I shall do.

I made a list of all the things I needed to do to settle my life as a widow. I committed to myself that I would harvest my inner strength to put my life in order. I had always encouraged young women who came to me by reassuring them that there was nothing they couldn't do if they set their minds to it. The first thing I had to do was sell the properties we owned so that I could buy or build something in Coimbatore where I had decided to stay. This was not an easy job but, after all, it was only a task that had to be completed.

I went to Delhi and waited outside our Patparganj flat, imploring the tenant with folded hands to return what was ours. I had hoped that reasoning with her, woman to woman, would work, but she banged the door shut on my face. Finally, with a good friend's help she was evicted. She had not paid rent for many years and the flat was our asset, bought for my and my husband's retirement. I immediately sold the flat because I did not have the will to rent it out again. I then sold the small property in Bangalore as well. I did not feel like living on my own and so far away from my mother. I did all this on my own. My husband's twinkling eyes and smile in my mind's eye spurred me on. I did not expect help from my children or my brothers and sisters, and I did not ask for any assistance either. I put my faith in God and my strength came from Guruvayoorappan and Sathya Sai Baba who were always in my heart.

One by one, I completed the items on the list I had made for myself. I sold my husband's old Fiat car and bought myself a small Maruti that I felt I could drive more easily. I was happy to have got a good value when I sold the Fiat. I feel proud of the strength I had to do things I had never done before. When my husband was alive, I had no idea about bank transactions or mutual funds. I would sign cheques that needed to be signed. But now I set up bank accounts and learned to think about savings and how to budget monthly expenses. I took Mediclaim insurance in case of future health needs. One day, I saw the name of a financial advisor in the paper. Her name was Bhagyam, which means luck, and I called her to the flat and asked her to help me invest with the savings I had.

The achievement I am most proud of was building my Lily Cottage in Kovaipudur, a beautiful suburb in the outskirts of the city and closer to Palakkad and my mother. I had always wanted an independent house and described my ideas to the architect, for him to draw on paper. Then I contacted a builder. The upper floor of the house had a separate entrance so that I could rent that portion and earn a monthly income. I thought it was an ingenious plan. The ground floor had a large room where I could gather my friends and devotees for Sai bhajans. This was something I always wanted to do. With god's grace, I managed it all on my own. My children had wanted me to buy a flat which would be safer and easier to maintain, but I needed to build this house with the front courtyard for the thulasi to grow and grace the house. This was a dream that I had had for a long time, and I was able to fulfil it.

I really enjoyed and appreciated my mother's frequent visits when she stayed with me in my Lily Cottage. We were both strong opinionated women. Though she didn't say it directly to me, I know that she was impressed by what I had built on my own. I lived in the house with only part-time help and drove the ninety-minute distance on my own to Mundarath to spend a few days with my mother every month. My three children made the effort to come from abroad every other year with their children and stayed with me in this house as well. But I had only lived a few years in my Lily Cottage when the house was robbed while I was away on a meditation retreat. I feel the watchman must have partnered with the thief to have planned this robbery so cleverly. Anyway, after that robbery, I did not have the courage to live in the house alone. Our past experience as landlords made me wary of renting the house to a tenant. I asked a friend to find me a buyer right away. Shashi thinks I made a point to build the place because I wanted to prove to myself that I could do it. He said that once I had done the job to my satisfaction, I sold the house. Perhaps he is right.

Lily enjoyed her years in Coimbatore. It was a place that she had found on her own, and it was the city in which she had the opportunity to live independently. The weather was more salubrious than in Kerala as the city was in the foothills of the hill-stations of Coonoor and Ooty. Fruits and vegetables were plentiful and more affordable than in the bigger metros. She felt that the people in Coimbatore were very helpful as well. She found a community at the Sai Centre, and she found her pleasure at the bookstore and with like-minded friends. She was pleased to set up a routine that included social connections, time for books, her daily communications with family and friends, and the opportunity to drive to Kollengode and Elevanchery with regularity. Of course, Coimbatore was a traditional city in Tamil Nadu and she had to get used to the raised eyebrows and the moniker she had earned of 'stylish *patti*' when she was dressed in her sleeveless summer blouses and drove all over town to run her errands!

Once Lily sold the Kovaipudur house, she had to find a new place and move. The children insisted that she enjoy the income she had generated from the sale of her Lily Cottage and not feel the burden of home ownership all over again. Lily rented a flat in a multi-storeyed building instead of looking for a home to purchase. She agreed that there was freedom and an ease of life in living in a multi-storeyed building with many amenities. 'You can just lock the front door and leave on a trip if you have to,' she said.

With her chatty personality and open-door nature, Lily soon became the go-to person in the building. All the younger women would stop by to share their stories of children's achievements or grievances about their husbands, or they would call on her to seek her advice on school admissions and travel. Lily enjoyed the company and cheerfully served as friend, philosopher and guide. The neighbours enjoyed the progressive thinking of Lily Tharoor and her flat was always open to visitors. Bhagyam's investment strategies were paying off as well. Lily was excited that this young woman who she had taken a chance on had proven to be so capable. Lily felt secure about the future. She planned to visit the children abroad every other year and the children agreed that they would come to India with her grandchildren in the years in between. She was thus assured of seeing them regularly.

Lily had full days and a busy routine in Coimbatore which is how she liked her life to be. She attended art classes and took Carnatic music lessons. She went often to the Sai center and attended bhajans every Thursday evening. She was often the lead singer at these gatherings. It made her happy and gave her peace of mind. She wrote down her pickle recipes and printed booklets of the recipes for friends. She began to cut household hints from newspapers and magazines to build a book of useful suggestions that she could print later or even publish. She drove to Mundarath once a month to see her mother and the siblings who lived in Elevanchery. Every year, she also travelled to Puttaparthi to be in the presence of her beloved Baba.

It was a life of her making, one that she chose and built on her own. As the years passed in Coimbatore without large ripples, many of Chandran and Lily's Malayalee friends from Calcutta began to head to South India for their retirement. The friends soon reconnected and they took turns meeting and visiting each other even if they lived in different south Indian towns. Annual retreats were planned and the Kolkata senior citizen group looked forward to holidays together in picturesque vacation spots. Lily was always game to join in outings and social events. During their get-togethers, some friends tried to coax Lily to consider the possibility of another life partner as she was still young, but Lily was resolute in her need to live her life on her own terms. And she was unafraid to do it alone. Lily's children were in regular touch with her, she still had a mother in her life, and she had grandchildren she loved. She felt that she had all that she wanted or needed.

Despite the grief that came from Chandran's absence, everything was looking up; proactive thoughts and actions reflect on all aspects of life. 'You learn a huge amount by opening yourself to things that are going on' was Lily's motto. She read widely at home and whenever she travelled. Though the children teased their mother that she didn't have a humorous bone in her body, Lily's favourite American author was humorist Erma Bombeck who wrote of suburban home life. And every time she visited California, she cherished the laugh aloud series of *The Golden Girls* and *I Love Lucy* that featured the careless, hilarious moments in Lucille Ball's life. In her own life, Lily echoed Lucille Ball's words, 'I'm not funny. What I am is brave.'

But once again, life and its usual ebb and flow had something different in store for Lily. Like the Y2K bug which was projected to create havoc in computer networks at the dawn of the 21st century, tumult in the personal lives of two of her children was imminent. Within a year of each other, Shashi and Smita's long established marriages had fractured. It was a painful time and Lily felt helpless and useless from afar. She missed her husband so much, especially his opinion and wisdom on many subjects. Though she recognized that sometimes living with a partner wasn't that easy, she knew that it was difficult to live without one, especially with little children in the home. It was hard for her to come to terms with the idea of divorce.

Lily wished to be strong for both her children but divorce is always a stressful and unsettling event. She felt fearful for her daughter who had three sons to raise on her own. Though she knew it was much harder for Smita and Shashi who were the ones going through the trauma, it was a stressful time for her as well. She was still in India and she had to answer questions from family and friends every day.

Years later, she would look back with pride at the personal and professional life Smita had built for herself, the love that she now had in her life and the fine young men she had raised. But, at the time, the dissolution of Shashi and Smita's long marriages affected Lily deeply and it was not easy for her to shake off the feeling of rootlessness. It sometimes made her feel the same insecurity that she had experienced every time Chandran's health showed signs of fragility.

But, as always, Lily pulled herself together. She continued to remain the strong independent matriarch that she had become. She was determined to fill the gap that the loss of the children's beloved daddy had rendered. She did not want to be 'a burden' to her children and she made sure that she would not become one. While there's life and good health, there is always hope. But though her energy was at full throttle, her arthritic knees were slowing her gait. She began to make enquiries for a reputable orthopaedic doctor in Coimbatore. Like Rabindranath Tagore's words that appeared so often in the magazine articles that she had read, 'If you cry because the sun has gone out of your life, your tears will prevent you from seeing the stars.' There still was much to be done, and she would do it. Her good health was important.

Purpose gives one focus and strength. For some it may be connected to their work while for others it may be in their responsibilities to their family. Some may find their purposeful meaning in their religious faith, and others in all of these aspects of life.

12

Good Innings

'When the winds of change blow, some people build walls, and others build windmills.'

—Anonymous proverb

Friends told me about Ganga Hospital and the excellent orthopaedic care that Dr Rajshekhar and his brother provided for knee and hip replacements. I was initially concerned about the proof of success of such a surgery as I had heard of cases where people were worse off after the procedure. I saw Prime Minister Vajpayee's shuffling gait on TV after he had his knees replaced, and I told my children that perhaps I would bear my knee pain a while longer. But they encouraged me to schedule the surgery and my daughters promised to come and be with me in the hospital so I would not have to go through the experience alone. I'm grateful that the knee replacement worked out as well as it did. Though I cannot sit on the floor anymore after the surgery, I can walk briskly all over again. It feels wonderful to have faced my doubts and fears.

In 2007, after finishing second in the 2006 selection for UN Secretary-General to Ban Ki-moon, Shashi announced his retirement from the United Nations. Of course, it was all politics and not popularity that influence these selections. Everybody thought Shashi should have won and become the next man at the top in the United Nations. He was so qualified and capable. It was quite disappointing for all of us, but I understood why my son did not want to stay on at the same place after the loss. He had been working at the United Nations since he was twenty-two. Many people got in touch with him with offers of employment and he accepted a position in a private company and continued to stay in New York City for his work. But I could see that my son was not very happy working in the private sector, doing tasks to help build the company's bottom line. He had spent all his life in public service. Shashi always said, 'India matters to me and I want to matter to India.' So, I was not all that surprised when he announced to the family that he was going to contest the Lok Sabha elections from Thiruvananthapuram as a Congress candidate.

I gave up my independent life in Coimbatore when Shashi returned to India in 2009 and joined politics. He said that he wanted me to live with him and my daughters too felt that I should not live alone anymore. After all, my son and I were both alone and we could be of strength to each other. I admit, I was at first vehemently against Shashi's interest in a political career. In India, many people think of politicians as corrupt people who join the field only to make money or make a name. My son was a highly educated scholarly man who spoke multiple languages and gave speeches in French and knew world leaders and heads of state. I saw politics as a fall from grace, but Shashi disabused me of this notion and told me that service to the nation is the highest of jobs. In fact, more educated people should embrace this path. I told him that he had worked hard enough all these years and did not need to enter this confused career at the expense of his health and reputation. But he was always an idealist like his father and thought he could make a difference in India. Shashi had returned from a comfortable life abroad for this life of service. What could I do other than help him in whatever way I could?

I made the move to Thiruvananthapuram in 2009 with some reluctance. But once I was there, and once the campaign started, I tried to be as useful as possible. My son's days began at sunrise and I set my alarm as well to greet the many people who came home with demands and suggestions. Even today, after all these years, my internal body alarm wakes me up at 5.30 a.m. since I used to wake up that early during the campaign.

So many interesting young people came from all over the world using their own money and time to volunteer for Shashi. They came because of their admiration of him and because they believed in the betterment of the nation. In his career in the UN, Shashi had demonstrated innovation, creativity, imagination and a willingness to create change and they all wanted to join in his efforts. The campaign was an education. Shashi was a political outsider and there was a lot of negative politics and personal attacks against him, but, with his direct and honest communication and friendly approach to people, and his belief in the values of secularism and pluralism, he had huge crowds gathering to hear his speeches.

Many people worked very hard at that time. Shobha came from America to support her brother and help during the campaign, making phone calls and addressing people. We are a close family and I am grateful that Shashi also had the support from his sons, nephews and his niece from afar. My brothers and sisters and my nephew joined to support Shashi and work on the ground during the campaign as well, even though their votes were elsewhere and in other constituencies. Smita too came from London after the campaign had ended and was able to stay for her brother's victorious election results. It was a proud moment for the family. Despite all the difficulties of the campaign, and the many naysayers stating that this newcomer would never win an election, Shashi won by a landslide of more than 1 lakh votes. He was elected as the new MP in the Lok Sabha from Thiruvananthapuram.

Though he may have been new in Indian politics, my son had had a long and successful career as a diplomat abroad. The Congress Party was aware of his achievements and made him a Minister of State for External Affairs. He was allocated a government bungalow in Delhi and he lived in Delhi for much of the time while I stayed on in Thiruvananthapuram.

2009 Victory Ride

Shashi was very close to his father and it was only after his return to India that he fully appreciated who his mother was and valued all that he had learned from her. He admitted in interviews that her ambition, her restlessness and what he once called in a book dedication—her 'divine discontent'— were all influences that had led him to strive and aspire. Lily's intellectual curiosity, her desire to know more about everything, her open and inquiring mind and her ability to navigate change were all inspiring qualities. Despite her consistent quarrel with his chosen career, Shashi began to rely on his mother's instincts and counsel. In his conversations with his sisters, he used to say, 'Mummy's tireless energy is an inspiration to me. Self-reliance is mummy's mantra. She doesn't like depending on others' help.'

Lily tried to embrace life in Thiruvananthapuram, but being the MP's mother didn't always make life easy. She disliked the lack of separation between home and work that the life of a politician seemed to entail. And it was clear to party workers and Shashi's staff that Lily disapproved of his long hours and the limitations of his personal or family time. Lily had little interest in politics and she wondered how she could give the best of her support to Shashi in those days. Though she would pat herself on her back when she felt deserving, she could also be her own strongest critic.

Yet, Lily had much to be proud of. She had begun life anew in another city in her seventies, accepted changes in her adult children's lives, came to terms with and even embraced new relationships and learnt new technology to stay connected. When a year later she saw that her son had found a life partner to be by his side who could support him in his life, she decided to move to Kochi to pick up the threads of her own independent life. Kochi was closer to Palakkad and to her mother whom she often visited.

Lily was ready to slow down her international travels but she had promised that she would see her daughters every year. So, if they were unable to come to India, she made the long journey required to travel to London and California. Lily was present with the rest of the family for every important occasion. She played a part in the marriage of her only granddaughter and blessed the couple by reciting a bhajan of Ganesha, the divine remover of obstacles, during the nuptials. A few years later, she made the journey for both grandsons' weddings and danced with abandon at their marriages in New York City and Richmond, VA. But each time she boarded the plane, she worried about how much things may change back home while she was away.

And she was right. On 24 June 2015, when Lily was with her daughter, grandchildren and great-granddaughter in California, she learned that her mother had left them. Jayashankini Amma was ninety-eight years old and just a few months short of starting the hundredth year of her life. Lily was devastated at being away from Kerala, but the family comforted her and said that the loss of this strong matriarch, who had kept the threads of the family tied together, was best borne in the company of her loved ones and not alone on her own in Kochi. Jayashankini Amma was a huge force and presence in the family and it seemed that the tharavad had shrunk in her absence. It felt like the end of an era in Lily's mind.

It was a difficult time in Shashi's life as well. He had become a widower, and the media onslaught and speculation regarding his wife's death was enough to destroy the sanity of almost anyone. Lily knew the strength and security she had felt when her mother was in her life, and she wished to provide something similar to Shashi. She wished to be his strength and stability as he navigated the rocky path of a political life in India without a partner by his side.

Lily was living on her own in her flat in Kochi. She read three newspapers every morning, borrowed magazines and books from a lending library, drove every day to the temple, stopped the car for her daily coconut water from the old man's stand under the tree and cooked for herself each morning, spreading dosa batter and grinding fresh coconut chutney. A part-time cleaner would come each day to tidy the house and restore the kitchen to some semblance of cleanliness. Lily also engaged with neighbours and friends and looked forward to the weekly 'Scrabble sessions' with her friend Irene who lived close by. It was a life she greatly enjoyed, but Shashi asked her multiple times to come and live with him. Though she held back on the move, it didn't stop her from climbing on to the campaign vehicle to stand by her son, even as recently as the third time he stood for election in 2019. And this was not the only exceptional thing she did. At eighty-two, she renewed her driving license and bought a new car. 'The old one is my wheelchair,' she remarked. 'I'll drive it on my daily errands.'

There is a powerful saying in Malayalam: 'swaram nannavumbol pattu Nirthuka', which means that one should stop singing before the voice is in decline (or stop when you are in your prime). But Lily had not reached that stage where she could no longer hold the note. Her strong voice and its call to action continued to fill the children's ears each day.

Driven individuals admire persistence and project power in their actions and their statements. They usually know what they want, they push beyond their comfort zone, and they are willing and interested in continuing to learn.

13

Age Is Only a Number

'Age is just a number. It's totally irrelevant unless, of course, you happen to be a bottle of wine.'

—Joan Collins

Now that I am in my bonus years, there are many things I've learned that I feel like sharing with others. I want to tell my friends and family that they shouldn't worry about the loss of material things. If someone takes something that was yours, it's okay; perhaps they needed it more than you did. I also want to say: don't wait to do the things you wish to do. If the opportunity you seek presents itself, embrace it right away and make it work for you. If there are people you have not seen in a while and you miss them, make the effort to see them now instead of waiting for tomorrow. I also know now that good sleep is so very essential for good health. My children never take naps, and my son still burns the midnight oil, but I tell them that good sleep at night can give you many more productive hours during the day. So many life's lessons come to us late. It's true that hindsight is 20/20.

And, one other fact that is certain is that age is only a number. Every year, we may get older; my children have celebrated all my significant birthdays since my husband passed away, with a cruise, with the glitter of Las Vegas and with tea with a Maharaja, but we don't have to become old. I used to visit my daughter's neighbour, Ann, in California and she was so full of energy at ninety. She lived alone and took care of all her personal needs without any help at all. And she was full of cheer and warmth. In fact, she told me that she was driving herself to the grocery store a year before my visit, but once her old car stopped on the road, and the waiting and inconveniences of repair took away her interest in keeping up the driver's license. I completely understand this. I have also bought a new car because I am afraid of car troubles with my old Maruti. And, since I'm no longer interested in learning to drive a new car, the children are happy that I have finally agreed to hire a driver for the new car when I go for my longer excursions. My Maruti is still with me and will be my 'wheelchair' when I am too tired or lazy to walk!

In the Western world, people think differently about age. Sophia Loren who is older than me, and whose movies I used to watch with my husband when we were in London, is still making movies and winning awards. She said, 'There is a fountain of youth: it is your mind, your talents, the creativity you bring to your life and the lives of people you love. When you learn to tap this source, you will truly have defeated age.' I like her approach to living and aging.

Lily's antidote to the boredom and loneliness that sometimes crept up with her own physical slowdown was the Internet. Though she missed the regular visits from her aging friends, who could no longer get around, there was a new world to explore online. She became a master of her computer, including signing on to daily Skype calls with her daughters in London and California. She learned from her grandson to find her favourite Malayalam serial *Vanambadi* and read the daily *Manaroma* news online during her travels away from India. She communicates with her relatives and friends on many continents using her smartphone. And though she occasionally forwards WhatsApp messages to a group rather than the intended individual, she recovers swiftly from the error! Lily lives the dictum that you are 'only as old as you allow yourself to feel'.

Informing and educating family members with forwards of YouTube videos and links to newspaper articles is a daily goal that Lily fulfils. A recent post on 'natural ways to fight dementia' was of particular interest to her as many old friends were showing signs of a cognitive slowdown. 'Brain-healthy vegetables to include in your diet are broccoli, avocado and red beets,' Lily writes at the top of the email.

As I type these words, I've just opened a forward from her about Bengaluru's (former Bangalore) latest innovation—idli on a stick for the person on the go who doesn't want to get his or her fingers dirty! She read Indra Nooyi's memoir hot off the press and was pleasantly surprised that Indra had a role in her home just like she did as a child: to light the *randal* at home in the evenings at sunset. She was reading Vir Sanghvi's memoir when I was with her last, and is certain to have some words to exchange with the author.

People who meet my mother, Lily, are always charmed and impressed by her quick mind and curiosity. She is not easily intimidated by title or rank, or by fame or fortune, and she speaks what is on her mind even if it displeases her children or grandchildren or even the guests who visit. But there is virtue in such true expression. Lily's instincts about people and situations usually hold water. In my brother Shashi's words, 'As she confidently soldiers on in her eighties, with two titanium knees, both eyes surgically freed of cataracts, but refusing to surrender to age, I feel an admiration welling up for her that I have rarely been able to express before. Her strength in coping with an early bereavement, independence of mind and body, faith in herself and determination to face life on her own are an extraordinary lesson.'

As Mummy often says to us, nothing remains young except the spirit. And for her, that curious spirit remains undisturbed and perhaps stronger in the slowness of older age. The evening of her life has a significance of its own.

Smita and I often laugh about the fact that when we were growing up, our mother used to sing out loud, 'Whatever you can do, I can do better!' It was not a goading taunt. It was an implicit call to action, a winking challenge and a reminder that she had years of experience from which we could learn. There are times even now that she uses the refrain. My siblings and I, we are chasing her still!

Afterword

This Too Is an Education

Ragini Tharoor Srinivasan

Some years ago, my grandmother—whom you have known in these pages as Lily, but whom I call Ammamma, my mother's mother—asked me to write her life story. I was her second choice.

A man in the business of ghostwriting other people's memoirs had come to her apartment for an interview. He planned to move to Thiruvananthapuram, where she was living at the time, and rent an apartment nearby. The two of them would speak every afternoon over tea. She was going to tell him her story, and he was going to write it for her. He pledged 150 pages in three months.

My mother and I exchanged emails with this writer. We asked him about his process. How did he plan to portray

Ammamma's distinct character? She wanted him to pay her for the right to tell her story. He expected her to pay him for serving as her scribe. We began to worry that anyone writing her story was going to end up injecting their own spirit into her words. In attempting to preserve her voice, they would inevitably produce their own. In the end, Ammamma said that he was too young anyway, and the deal was off.

The task of writing her book then fell to me. Although ours is a family full of writers, I am the only granddaughter ('the one and only', she says). Since my student life at the time was relatively unencumbered, and Ammamma and I are very close, I recorded some interviews on my iPod. I sent her questions by email. We made a few false starts. A decade passed. Ammamma's reticence to share her story and ambivalence about self-disclosure—first, because her mother was still alive, and then because of fears of distracting from her son's career—became both of our alibis for not working on the book, though she desperately wanted it written. How I worried that it would never happen! That she would not live to hear her story told.

And now it's finally here—the book of Ammamma's life, not late at all, but right on time. In the words of poet W.S. Merwin, 'The right time after all / not according to / however we planned it.'

The story of Ammamma's extraordinary, ordinary journey is written, exactly as it was meant to be told, by her daughter, my mother. At the level of genre, *Good Innings* is a hybrid text. It is both a biography of Lily Tharoor and a work of creative nonfiction by Shobha Tharoor Srinivasan, constellated with citations from multiple languages, texts and thinkers whose words of wisdom uncannily speak Ammamma's own life philosophy. *Good Innings* is also a self-help book, at least to the extent that, in Mohsin Hamid's playful words, 'All books, each and every book ever written, could be said to be offered to the reader as a form of self-help.'[*]

What you have encountered in the preceding chapters is both a single-authored work and a co-creative project between Lily and Shobha, a lifetime in the making. The accessible, forward-looking, propulsive prose of the book matches Lily's open, forward-thinking, energetic approach to living. Those who know Lily will recognize her in these pages; those who do not know her may hear in her story echoes of their own.

With *Good Innings,* my mother has managed the impossible alchemy of capturing Ammamma's spirit and voice without either ventriloquizing her, on the one hand, or speaking over her, on the other. What is offered in these pages is nothing less than what the feminist theorist Trinh T. Minh-ha calls 'speaking nearby', which is a form of speaking 'that reflects on itself and can come very close to a subject without, however, seizing or claiming it.'[†] Speaking nearby

---

[*] Mohsin Hamid, *How to Get Filthy Rich in Rising Asia* (Riverhead Books, 2013), p. 20.

[†] Nancy N. Chen, '"Speaking Nearby": A Conversation with Trinh T. Minh-ha,' *Visual Anthropology Review* Vol. 8, No. 1 (Spring 1992), p. 87.

requires both ethical distance and intimate proximity. It requires knowledge and careful thinking, both about what is to be said and what is to be left unspoken. In the words of anthropologist Anand Pandian, who co-wrote a hybrid work of memoir-ethnography with his grandfather, M.P. Mariappan, 'This kind of thinking has to be done with care.'* Ultimately, it is a practice of love.

My grandmother is an ambitious woman. She has been ambitious for herself, as you will have discovered in reading this book, and she is ambitious for those around her. We who have been the focus of her attention sometimes chafe against all that desire and drive, her congenital restlessness and exuberance. I believe now that Ammamma probably didn't want me to write her story; she just wanted me to invest in my own. In the end, she didn't need me, because the right person, at the right moment, who understood the full context, rose to the occasion. The Greeks have a name for this radical timeliness; they call it *kairos*. I offer one more enabling term: 'daughter'.

Ammamma often laments that she was not born in her children's or grandchildren's generation. If she'd had our educations, she says, she would have been on top of the world. She would have reached heights higher even than Ambani's Antilia. 'I am from the village,' she says, 'and with my background, and my knowledge and education, and

---

* Anand Pandian and M.P. Mariappan, *Ayya's Accounts: A Ledger of Hope in Modern India* (Indiana University Press, 2014), p. 8.

coming from my way, with my limited exposure, I have made so much of my life.'

This conviction is what brought the ghostwriter to Ammamma's door all those years ago. This is why Penguin approached my mother to write her story. And this is what I hope you, her reader, will leave with as well: if not the belief that you have lived your life to the best of your ability, then the resolution to do so in the years to come; if not pride in what you have made of your own circumstances, then forgiveness for whatever your shortcomings.

A final word to my Ammamma, whose book this is. The love and good faith in these chapters are a credit and tribute to you. When you read them, I hope you say to yourself what you have had occasion to say before, and what you have taught me to strive to say, at the end of the day, against whatever odds: 'I am giving myself pat on my back. I am saying I DID MANAGE WELL'.

Acknowledgements

This book would not have been written if Premanka Goswami of Penguin India had not called, emailed and persistently persuaded me to tell my mother's story. My thanks to him, Aparna Kumar, Aparna Abhijit and to the rest of the Penguin team for their support at every stage of bringing this book to fruition.

My gratitude to my brother, Shashi, for not accepting my excuse of a 'full plate' and for always encouraging me to pursue new achievements. His thoughtful feedback on the early draft helped fill in gaps on dates and timelines. I thank my sister, Smita, for sending me recorded clips of conversations with our mother that she gathered patiently each day during her 2020 lockdown in Delhi. Her enthusiasm for everything I do embellishes my creativity. My go-to person in our ancestral home, my uncle, Mukundan, with whom I share fond childhood memories, read the early chapters and helped with names and details. This book could not be what it is without my daughter Ragini—my strength, my support, my strongest critic and my steady muse. Her presence and the Afterword to this book bring the family and these words together.

Finally, my thanks to my father, Chandran, who first recognized the author in me and whose regular letters encouraged my own writing, and to my mother, Lily, for inspiring us through her life and living, and without whom there would have been no story to tell.

Glossary

A

Aarattu festival: An aaru in Malayalam is a body of water (usually a river or lake) and the Aarattu festival is the festival when the temple deity is taken to the water for a ritual bathing. The festival is celebrated twice each year in Kerala, usually in the months of October–November, and again in the months of April–May

Ammamma: mother's mother, maternal grandmother

Archanas: a special puja and offering to a deity performed by a temple priest

Ashtapadi: Sanskrit hymns from the Gita Govinda that describe the beauty of Lord Krishna and the love between Krishna and the gopis

C

Chechi: older sister

'Chetta po, shivodi va': 'Chetta' in Malayalam is a colloquial term for rubbish. 'Shivodi' is the Bhagawati or female god and 'va' is a call to come

Cherriamas: aunts; mother's younger sisters

Chorunnu: A young child's first rice-eating ceremony

D

Desavilaku: an annual temple festival in Kerala when all temple lamps (vilakus) are lit. The festivals happen in different counties or 'desams'

E

Edathiamma: sister-in-law (Older brother's wife. The younger brother's wife is usually addressed by her name

Etta: older brother (short form of *chettan* in Malayalam)

G

Guruvayoorappan: Guruvayoorappan is a manifestation of Lord Vishnu and is worshipped in Kerala. He is the presiding deity of the Guruvayur temple

H

Housie-Housie: Bingo. It is a game of chance where tickets or cards containing numbered squares are matched by participants to numbers that are randomly selected and called out by an announcer

K

Karanavar: male head in a Malayalee/Malayali tharavad

Karkada Sankranti: On the first day of the Malayalam month of Karkada, homes are thoroughly cleaned and the Bhagawati is decorated and dressed in silk and placed in the front room of the house where the family gathers to read aloud from the Ramayana

Karyastan: the caretaker of a property

Kollen: Malayalam word for blacksmith

Kondatam: dried vegetables and rice flour snacks that can be fried and eaten with a meal (like papad)

'*Koodi koodi varuntha lavanyam*': these words from an advertisement translate to 'the radiance and beauty that continues to increase'. Since this was the refrain for a Malayalam commercial, the product was most likely a body soap

Krishi: rice paddy field.

M

Mama: maternal uncle

Marumakkathayam: a matrilineal system of inheritance; Marumakkathayam is the practice of inheriting lineage and assets from the mother's family

Muttam: front courtyard

Murukku: a savory, crunchy snack shaped in a coiled circle that is made with rice and urud dal flour (similar to a *chakli* in shape but gram flour is not used)

Muthashi: grandmother

N

Nalukettu or Ettukettu: These were the traditional house constructions and architectural style in Kerala. The homes would have either four wings around an inner courtyard (nadu mittam) or eight wings around two nadu mittams. The sections/wings enclosed a central atrium/inner courtyard

Neyyu: butter which is churned from butter milk at home. This was later heated and made into clarified butter (ghee)

O

Ottamthullal: a dance and poetry art form of Kerala in which the dancer also recites as he performs

P

Patti: Tamil term usually for grandmother but can also be used for an older woman

Pottu: bindi (a coloured dot on the forehead)

Pavada davini: Long skirt and dupatta draped like a half-sari. This was usually worn in south India during the transitional age (teenage years) from childhood to adulthood

R

Randal: hurricane lamp

S

Seetharkundu: Is believed to be the waters in which Sita had bathed during the *vanavasam* (the years of dwelling in the forest during their exile) with Rama and Lakshmana

T

Tharavad: Ancestral home
Thottil: Hammock often constructed using sarees.

U

Unni: small child—this is a tender term. Many boys in Kerala were called unni. (Like 'khoka' as a 'daak naam' in Bengal)

V

Valliama: The term used for an aunt who is older than the parent, (mother or father) or the wife of the father's older brother, (valliachen). The term is especially used in Palakkad and the Malabar area of Kerala
Valiyamaman: male elder of the tharavad. Usually the mother's uncle
Vilaku: lamp